THE ROLE OF NATIONAL HUMAN RIGHTS INSTITUTIONS AT THE INTERNATIONAL AND REGIONAL LEVELS

National Human Rights Institutions (NHRIs), defined by the UN as bodies established to promote and protect human rights, have increased in number since the General Assembly adopted principles governing their effectiveness in 1993. The UN and others have encouraged states to set up such institutions as an indication of their commitment to human rights, and now over 20 such institutions exist in Africa and many more will follow. These institutions have taken various forms including ombudsmen, commissions, or a combination of the two. They differ in terms of how they are established; some by constitution, some by legislation and some by decree. These NHRIs have varying functions, usually both promotional and protective, such as giving advice to government, parliament, and others, making recommendations on compliance with human rights standards, awareness raising, and analysis of law and policy. Despite the considerable variations in the method of their creation, powers and composition, most of these institutions have chosen or indeed been mandated, to become involved in international and regional fora. This book examines these institutions in the African region, the way in which they use the international and regional fora, the effectiveness of their contributions and how they are able to participate.

Human Rights Law in Perspective : Volume 11

Human Rights Law in Perspective

General Editor: Colin Harvey

The language of human rights figures prominently in legal and political debates at the national, regional and international levels. In the UK the Human Rights Act 1998 has generated considerable interest in the law of human rights. It will continue to provoke much debate in the legal community and the search for original insights and new materials will intensify.

The aim of this series is to provide a forum for scholarly reflection on all aspects of the law of human rights. The series will encourage work which engages with the theoretical, comparative and international dimensions of human rights law. The primary aim is to publish over time books which offer an insight into human rights law in its contextual setting. The objective is to promote an understanding of the nature and impact of human rights law. The series is inclusive, in the sense that all perspectives in legal scholarship are welcome. It will incorporate the work of new and established scholars.

Human Rights Law in Perspective is not confined to consideration of the UK. It will strive to reflect comparative, regional and international perspectives. Work which focuses on human rights law in other states will therefore be included in this series. The intention is to offer an inclusive intellectual home for significant scholarly contributions to human rights law.

Volume 1 Importing the Law in Post-Communist Transitions
Catherine Dupré

Volume 2 The Development of the Positive Obligations Under the European Convention on Human Rights by the European Court of Human Rights
Alastair Mowbray

Volume 3 Human Rights Brought Home: Socio-Legal Studies of Human Rights in the National Context
Edited by Simon Halliday and Patrick Schmidt

Volume 4 Corporations and Transnational Human Rights Litigation
Sarah Joseph

Volume 5 Human Rights in the Community: Rights as Agents for Change
Edited by Colin Harvey

Volume 6 Human Rights, Culture and the Rule of Law
Jessica Almqvist

Volume 7 Property and the Human Rights Act 1998
Tom Allen

Volume 8 Gender, Culture and Human Rights
Siobhán Mullally

Volume 9 Monetary Remedies for Breach of Human Rights
Lisa Tortell

Volume 10 Judicial Review, Socio-Economic Rights and the Human Rights Act
Ellie Palmer

The Role of National Human Rights Institutions at the International and Regional Levels

The Experience of Africa

Rachel Murray

•HART•
PUBLISHING

OXFORD AND PORTLAND, OREGON
2007

Published in North America (US and Canada) by
Hart Publishing
c/o International Specialized Book Services
920 NE 58th Avenue, Suite 300
Portland, OR 97213-3786
USA
Tel: +1 503 287 3093 or toll-free: (1) 800 944 6190
Fax: +1 503 280 8832
E-mail: orders@isbs.com
Website: www.isbs.com

Hart Publishing, 16C Worcester Place, OX1 2JW
Telephone: +44 (0)1865 517530 Fax: +44 (0)1865 510710
E-mail: mail@hartpub.co.uk
Website: http://www.hartpub.co.uk

British Library Cataloguing in Publication Data
Data Available

ISBN-13: 978-1-84113-394-2 (hardback)

Typeset by Hope Services, Abingdon
Printed and bound in Great Britain by
TJI Digital, Padstow, Cornwall

Acknowledgements

This book is a much better product due to the involvement of a number of people. First, the Socio-Legal Studies Association (SLSA) provided funding to enable me to visit the UN in Geneva and crucially to observe the 17th session of the International Coordinating Committee of National Human Rights Institutions. Marianne Haugaard and Orest Nowosad were particularly helpful in facilitating my access to this forum and in providing me with relevant documentation. I am also grateful for discussions I had with Alpha Connelly (Irish Human Rights Commission), Bukhari Bello (then Executive Secretary of the Nigerian National Human Rights Commission) and Catherine Mumma (Kenya National Human Rights Commission).

Funding from the SLSA also enabled a trip to be made to South Africa to speak to members of the South African Human Rights Commission and the Secretariat of the African National Human Rights Institutions. I am very grateful to Bharat Malkani for undertaking this trip on my behalf, conducting the relevant interviews and taking useful and readable notes. I would also like to thank Tseliso Thipanyane from the South African Human Rights Commission for agreeing to be interviewed.

I am very grateful to those who took time to read earlier drafts of this book, providing me with useful feedback and comments. Thanks to Tonia Novitz and Tony Prosser, as well as, in particular, Ibrahima Kane for their invaluable views.

The African Commission on Human and Peoples' Rights has continued to provide me with access to its sessions and without its former documentalist, Jan Jalloh, I would have been unable to obtain many of the documents used here. In addition, I am also very grateful to Ben Kioko at the AU in Addis Ababa for providing relevant material.

Given that this book has taken rather longer than I initially envisaged, I would like to thank Richard Hart for his patience and understanding, and particularly for accommodating my initial delays and changes to his timetable.

Rachel Murray
January 2007

Contents

Abbreviations

ACHPR	African Charter on Human and Peoples' Rights
ANHRI	African National Human Rights Institutions
AU	African Union
CCANI	Coordinating Committee of African National Human Rights Institutions
CEDAW	United Nations Convention on the Elimination of All Forms of Discrimination Against Women
ECOSOC	United Nation's Economic and Social Council
ECOSOCC	African Union's Economic, Social and Cultural Council
ECOWAS	Economic Community of West African States
ICC	International Coordinating Committee of National Human Rights Institutions
ICCPR	International Covenant on Civil and Political Rights
ICERD	Committee on the Elimination of Racial Discrimination
ICESCR	International Covenant on Economic, Social and Cultural Rights
ICHRP	International Council on Human Rights Policy
NGOs	Non-Governmental Organisations
NHRI	National Human Rights Institution
OAU	Organization of African Unity
OHCHR	Office of the United Nations High Commissioner for Human Rights
OPCAT	Optional Protocol to the UN Convention Against Torture
UDHR	Universal Declaration of Human Rights
UNCAT	United Nations Committee Against Torture
UNCRC	United Nations Committee on the Rights of the Child
UNDP	United Nations Development Programme
UNICEF	United Nations Children's Fund

1

The Role of National Human Rights Institutions at the International and Regional Levels

INTRODUCTION

NATIONAL HUMAN RIGHTS Institutions (NHRIs), namely those defined by the UN as 'a body which is established by a government under the constitution, or by law or decree, the functions of which are specifically defined in terms of the promotion and protection of human rights,'[1] have increased in number since the UN General Assembly adopted principles governing their effectiveness in 1993.[2] The UN and others have encouraged states to set up such institutions as an indication of their commitment to human rights and now over twenty such institutions exist in Africa[3] and where none

[1] United Nations, *National Human Rights Institutions. A Handbook on the Establishment and Strengthening of National Institutions for the Promotion and Protection of Human Rights*, Professional Training Series No 4, 1995, at para 39.

[2] Principles Relating to the Status and Functioning of National Institutions for the Protection and Promotion of Human Rights (The Paris Principles), Resolution 1992/54, endorsed by UN General Assembly Resolution 48/134, 20 December 1993, Annex.

[3] These include Algeria's Commission Nationale des Droits de l'Homme, Commission Béninoise des Droits de l'Homme, Burkina Faso Commission Nationale des Droits de l'Homme, Haut Commissariat aux droits de l'homme et a la bonne gouvernance of Central African Republic, Cameroon National Commission on Human Rights and Freedoms, Chad's Commission Nationale des Droits de l'Homme, Democratic Republic of Congo's Observatoire Nationale des Droits de l'Homme, Egypt's National Council for Human Rights, Gabon's National Human Rights Commission, Ghana's Commission on Human Rights and Administrative Justice, Kenya Human Rights Commission, Madagascar National Human Rights Commission, Malawi Human Rights Commission, Mauritania's Commissariat des Droits de l'Homme à la Lutte contre la Pauvreté et la Insertion, Mauritius Commission Nationale des Droits de l'Homme, Morocco Conseil Consultatif des Droits de l'Homme, Namibia Office of the Ombudsman, Niger Commission Nationale Des Droits de l'Homme et des Libertés Fondamentales, Nigerian Human Rights Commission, Commission Rwandaise des Droits de l'Homme, Comité Sénégalaise des Droits de l'Homme, South African Human Rights Commission, Tanzanian Commission for Human Rights and Good Governance, Togo Commission Nationale des Droits de l'Homme, Tunisia Higher Committee on Human Rights and Fundamental Freedoms, Uganda Human Rights Commission, Zambian Permanent Human Rights Commission. See earlier discussion on some of these: Human Rights Watch, *Protectors or Pretenders? Government Human Rights Commissions in Africa* (New York, Human Rights Watch, 2001).

exist, those states across the African continent and the world have recently chosen to[4] or are considering doing so.[5]

These institutions have taken various forms including ombudsmen, commissions, or a combination of the two.[6] They differ in terms of how they are established, some by constitution,[7] some by legislation[8] and some by decree.[9] Appointment of their members, some of whom are the sole Commissioner as in Ghana,[10] others who form a team of over ten, on full and part time bases, can be done by the legislature,[11] the government,[12] or a combination of the two. These NHRIs have varying functions, usually both promotional and protective, such as giving advice to government, parliament, and others, making recommendations on compliance with human rights standards, awareness raising, and analysis of law and policy. Some, such as the Ghanaian Commission on Human Rights and Administrative Justice have the power to examine complaints,[13] some can undertake visits to places of detention.[14]

Despite these considerable variations in the method of their creation, powers and composition, most of these institutions have chosen or indeed been mandated, to become involved in international and regional forums. There has been very little attention in literature to the way in which NHRIs use these forums, the effectiveness of their contributions and how they are able to participate. This book seeks to fill the gap. By looking at the African region, the book aims to analyse what role African NHRIs play at the international and regional levels.

Studies on African NHRIs indicate various concerns with their operation. For example, the important Human Rights Watch report in 2001, *Protectors or*

[4] Eg in Angola, Sudan and Liberia, see Commission on Human Rights, *Effective Functioning of Human Rights Mechanisms: National Institutions and Regional Arrangements*, Report of the Secretary-General, E/CN.4/2006/101, 24 January 2006, paras 35, 36 and 40.

[5] Eg Zimbabwe is considering establishing a national human rights institution, see 'Human Rights Body Gets Nod' *The Sunday Mail*, 26 March 2006, http://www.sundaymail.co.zw/inside.aspx?sectid=365&cat=12.; in the Federation of Comoros, a bill concerning the creation of a Commission Nationale des Droits de l'Homme is being discussed by the National Assembly. For examples in other states see also: United Nations Office of the High Commissioner for Human Rights (OHCHR), Africa Region, Quarterly Reports of Field Offices, March 2005, at 25.

[6] Eg, Ghana's Commission on Human Rights and Administrative Justice (CHRAJ) fused a Human Rights Commission, an Ombudsman and an Anti-Corruption Agency, Commission on Human Rights and Administrative Justice Act 1993, Act 456 of 6 July 1993.

[7] Eg South African Human Rights Commission, firstly by the interim Constitution of 1993, then consolidated in the final Constitution of 1997, s 184.

[8] Eg Ghana's Commission on Human Rights and Administrative Justice, Commission on Human Rights and Administrative Justice Act 1993, Act 456 of 6 July 1993; Nigeria's National Commission on Human Rights, Human Rights Commission Act 1995.

[9] Eg the Nigerian National Human Rights Commission, Human Rights Commission Act 1995.

[10] Supported by two deputy Commissioners.

[11] As in the case of the Kenya Human Rights Commission, Kenya National Commission on Human Rights Act 2002, s 4(1) which provides that nine Commissioners are to be nominated by the National Assembly and then appointed by the President. The Chair of the Commission is appointed from among the Commissioners.

[12] Eg the members of the Mauritanian Commissariat aux Droits de l'Homme à la lutte contre la Pauvreté et à l'Insertion, decree of 2 July 1998, Arts 4 and 7.

[13] As does, for example, the Nigerian National Human Rights Commission.

[14] Eg Uganda Human Rights Commission, Nigerian Human Rights Commission.

Pretenders?[15] considered a number of institutions on the continent and concluded that although at that stage they are,

> a mixed bag. Given the needs of their societies, to date the performance of most has been disappointing. . . . Unfortunately, even where human rights commissions in Africa function reasonably well, they have their limitations. . . . It is noticeable, in fact, how the national commissions in Cameroon, Chad and Togo, among others, have become less outspoken over the years due to government pressures and how the commissions in Benin and Senegal, for example, have been less active than might have been expected given the generally positive political climates in which they are able to operate. By contrast, certain other commissions have achieved a relatively strong record of inactivity in much less favourable political conditions.[16]

There are various reasons why a government may choose to establish an NHRI in its country. It may be part of wider constitutional change, as in South Africa; it may be an indication of the government's commitment to human rights, as in Ghana, Malawi and Senegal,[17] or as a defence to criticisms over its human rights record, as was the case in Nigeria[18] and more recently in Zimbabwe.[19] The possibility of external funding for such bodies, from the (United Nations Development Programme (UNDP)[20] or other donors,[21] may also be an incentive.

The thrust of the approach of the UN, its agencies, particularly the UNDP, the African Commission on Human and Peoples' Rights and others has been that NHRIs are a good thing that should be encouraged, thereby advocating the establishment of NHRIs in countries where none exist and being prepared to

[15] Above n 3.

[16] Ibid, at 4–5. Similarly, see J Matshekga, 'Toothless Bulldogs? The Human Rights Commissions of Uganda and South Africa: A Comparative Study of their Independence' (2002) 2(1) *African Human Rights Law Journal* 68–91; A Makubuya, 'Breaking the Silence: A Review of the Maiden Report of the Uganda Human Rights Commission' (1999) 5 *East African Journal of Peace and Human Rights* 213; J Hatchard, 'A New Breed of Institution: The Development of Human Rights Commissions in Commonwealth Africa with particular Reference to the Uganda Human Rights Commission' (1999) *Comparative and International Law Journal of South Africa* 28; OC Okafor and SC Agbakwa, 'On Legalism, Popular Agency and "Voices of Suffering": The Nigerian National Human Rights Commission in Context' (2002) 24 *Human Rights Quarterly* 662–720.

[17] Human Rights Watch, above n 3, at 29.

[18] AMO Obe, 'Working with National Human Rights Commissions. The Experience of Nigeria' www.scu.edu.tw/hr/research_imgs/Ayo.pdf.

[19] See above, n.5 .

[20] 'Supporting national human rights institutions has been one of UNDP's priorities in a number of countries, most often countries with challenging political environments. UNDP's support to national human rights institutions can be clustered under two phases: (1) the pre-establishment phase; and (2) the consolidation phase', Statement of United Nations Development Programme (UNDP) to 61st Session of the UN Commission on Human Rights. See discussion of UNDP role in Human Rights Watch, above n 3, at 77–78.

[21] 'International donor pressure and financial support for human rights commissions has been the impetus for African governments to create human rights commissions, in part to reassure donors of their commitment to human rights. For example, both the Kenyan and Zambian human rights commissions were created shortly before donor meetings to discuss renewal of aid conditioned on human rights and economic reforms. International funding is increasingly available to governments who announce their intention to create a human rights commission,' ibid, at 76.

support those already functioning even if they have dubious credentials.[22] This has not been matched by any systematic consideration of whether it may be appropriate to have an NHRI in that particular jurisdiction, or a detailed analysis of the effectiveness of many of these institutions.

What consideration is undertaken of these issues centres around compliance with the Paris Principles. The 1993 Paris Principles provide for competence and responsibilities of such institutions, including that they have 'as broad a mandate as possible' and detailing a number of responsibilities from giving advice to government, parliament and others, examining legislation and administrative measures for their compliance with human rights standards, considering violations, preparing reports on human rights matters, reacting to events, teaching and research and publicising forms of discrimination. They contain a number of provisions outlining what NHRIs could do at the international level, such as encouraging states to ratify relevant treaties, contributing to reporting procedures and co-operating with international and regional bodies. The Principles also suggest ways in which the state can guarantee the independence of the NHRI, from ensuring that the appointment of its members reflects a variety of representation of different sectors of society, that it has funding to enable it to operate effectively and independently and that there is some stable mandate in their appointment. Methods of how an NHRI should operate include that it freely considers issues that fall within its competence; is able to hear individuals and obtain necessary documents; makes public statements, through the media if necessary; meets regularly, and establishes working groups and consults with others, particularly with NGOs. For those NHRIs which have 'quasi-jurisdictional competence,'-namely the ability to hear complaints of violations—the Principles state that such NHRIs could include powers to come to amicable settlements, inform the parties of their rights, hear the complaint or transfer it to another authority and make recommendations to relevant bodies.

These Principles have been taken as the benchmark against which NHRIs have been assessed. They are referred to at the national, regional and international levels as the standards to which governments should adhere when considering the establishment of such bodies, and are central to discussions at the international and regional levels concerning the role that NHRIs play there.

Despite this, they are a crude instrument in assessing the effectiveness of NHRIs. Research has shown that many factors impact on whether an NHRI can operate effectively and have a positive impact in promoting and protecting human rights.[23] These include not only factors dealt with by the Paris Principles such as the conditions under which it is created, namely how its members are

[22] 'UNDP has given funding to some of the least credible human rights commissions on the African continent, and is not providing support to all of the strong or promising human rights commissions in Africa,' ibid, at 78.

[23] S Livingstone and R Murray, *Evaluating the Effectiveness of National Human Rights Institutions: The Northern Ireland Human Rights Commission and Comparisons with South Africa*, 2005, on file with author.

appointed, whether it is established by legislature or constitution, who is chosen to sit on the NHRI, but takes into account how the institution performs. Does it have a strategy? Does it use its money and powers effectively and to their full extent? Does it have an appropriate media and communication strategy and a coherent organisation and managerial structure? Furthermore, it is also necessary to examine the effectiveness of an NHRI in light of how it is perceived by others, whether that is government, the legislative, civil society, media, or the wider public. It is a combination of all these factors which renders an NHRI effective.[24] While some of these are in the control of government, others, particularly if they do in fact operate separately from government influence, will be dependent on the NHRI itself. As will be seen in chapter 6, whether one holds a government or an NHRI itself accountable for the NHRI's activities should, ideally, depend on what particular aspect of the NHRI is being considered. Yet, the model adopted by the UN and regional bodies is not to probe that closely into how an NHRI operates, but simply to take the Paris Principles as the checklist against which they should be assessed and the extent of their participation in international and regional forums determined.

INDEPENDENCE

In order to be an effective watchdog on government it is argued that NHRIs must be independent from government. The Paris Principles have a specific section on 'composition and guarantees of independence and pluralism' which includes:

> The national institution shall have an infrastructure which is suited to the smooth conduct of its activities, in particular adequate funding. The purpose of this funding should be to enable it to have its own staff and premises, in order to be independent of the Government and not be subject to financial control which might affect its independence. In order to ensure a stable mandate for the members of the national institution, without which there can be no real independence, their appointment shall be effected by an official act which shall establish the specific duration of the mandate. This mandate may be renewable, provided that the pluralism of the institution's membership is ensured.[25]

The very nature of an NHRI, however, is that its establishment at the very least requires government commitment and involvement. NHRIs obtain their very influence by the fact that, unlike NGOs, they are official bodies that have a constitutional or statutory status but which, at the same time, are able to operate separately from government. The notion of independence is a difficult one to define. Dictionary definitions suggest 'freedom from the influence or control of others,' namely not depending on another for financial support. While the Paris

[24] Ibid.
[25] Paris Principles, paras B(2) and (3).

Principles capture certain elements of this, they do not reflect the subtleties of the relationship that an NHRI should have with government. Indeed, it is crucial if the NHRI is to have any impact that it operates on an inside track with government and is respected by it and brought into its trust.[26] NHRIs are different from NGOs because they are presumed to occupy some semi-official position. On the other hand, an NHRI is presumed to be the watchdog of government and in order to do so, must not be in the pocket of government; it must ideally have integrity to step back and make decisions alone which may conflict with the views of government:

> While the aim of the Paris Principles is to ensure as much autonomy from government, particularly the executive, in practice most commissions find it difficult to maintain such a distance. This is, in a way, both a strength and a weakness. By being close to or a part of government, a commission may lend legitimacy to the notion of human rights, whether or not this accords with the state's intention. Even in the most repressive regimes, the establishment of an official state body devoted to human rights may, on occasion, create an official space for a human rights discourse and may foster greater, even if limited, activism and awareness. . . . And if a state sponsored national human rights commission issues a hard-hitting statement or document, so officially acknowledging that a particular problem exists or abuse has taken place, it can be much more difficult for a government to dismiss than, say a similar statements or report issued by a local or international NGO.[27]

How NHRIs themselves tread this difficult line and for what they should be accountable has not been fully explored by the UN or African bodies.

Independence in terms of the Paris Principles is usually equated with independence from government. But it is clear that to be effective an NHRI should also be able to co-operate without succumbing to pressure from other actors, whether that be NGOs, parliamentarians or other statutory agencies, for example. But this is an issue that is not applied by the UN and regional bodies when examining an NHRI's independence. Furthermore, it is also essential that NHRIs work closely with all these other actors in order to have any impact on human rights in their society. As it is inevitably linked to government, the NHRI can be viewed with suspicion by civil society and others. As Human Rights Watch note:

> The proliferation of national human rights commissions, with many established in repressive states, poses something of a dilemma for human rights activists who are more accustomed to challenging the state on rights issues than collaborating with it. For them and others, the question to be considered is: are such state-sponsored human rights bodies to be regarded with suspicion and distrust or should their development be encouraged and supported?.[28]

[26] Livingstone and Murray, above n 23.
[27] Human Rights Watch, above n 3, at 3.
[28] Ibid, at 1.

As this book will discuss, the notion of independence is cited as central to the effectiveness of an NHRI and therefore the extent to which it should be able to participate at the level of the UN and regionally, and yet it is not an issue that has been discussed in great detail. The ways in which the UN and regional bodies have approached this concept of independence is therefore not particularly satisfactory. In part because NHRIsare relatively new institutions, and in part because the issue of independence is not satisfactorily resolved at the national level, this tension has been played out at the international and regional levels. This becomes apparent in a number of ways such as where NHRIs have sat in meetings[29] and what their role is perceived to be-are they part of state apparatus and thus assessed along with state commitments or are they part of the supervisory mechanisms to keep a check on government compliance with international obligations?[30]

THE SCOPE OF THIS STUDY

Although there has been considerable research done on NHRIs,[31] less has looked at either specific institutions,[32] or specific parts of an NHRI's mandate. Despite the very similar roles that these institutions play, and powers they possess, and although various seminars and workshops have brought NHRIs and others together to discuss examples of best practice,[33] there has been little critical analysis of the effectiveness of such bodies in respect of any of these particular functions.

The Paris Principles advocate that NHRIs should have 'as broad a mandate as possible.' Within this, considerable attention is paid by the Paris Principles to the international role that NHRIs can play. Thus, they advocate that among the responsibilities an NHRI should have, it should:

(b) promote and ensure the harmonization of national legislation regulations and practices with the international human rights instruments to which the State is a party, and their effective implementation;

[29] See, eg J Black, 'Regulatory Conversations' (2002) 29(1) *Journal of Law and Society* 163–96.

[30] See chs 2 and 6 below.

[31] Eg Commonwealth Secretariat, *National Human Rights Institutions. Best Practice* (London, Commonwealth Secretariat, 2001); K Hossain, L Besselink, H Selaisse and E Volker (eds), *National Human Rights Commissions and Ombudsman Offices: National Experiences Throughout the World* (Dordrecht, Kluwer Law International, 2001); Human Rights Watch, above n 3; International Council on Human Rights Policy, *Performance and Legitimacy: National Human Rights Institutions* (Geneva, ICHRP, 2000); International Council on Human Rights Policy, *Assessing the Effectiveness of National Human Rights Institutions* (Geneva, International Council on Human Rights Policy, Office of the UN High Commissioner for Human Rights, 2005); Livingstone and Murray, above n 23; S Livingstone and R Murray, 'The Effectiveness of National Human Rights Institutions' in S Halliday and P Schmidt (eds), *Human Rights Brought Home: Socio Legal Perspectives on Human Rights in the National Context* (Oxford, Hart Publishing, 2004) 137–64; LC Reif, 'Building Democratic Institutions: The Role of National Human Rights Institutions in Good Governance and Human Rights Protection, (2000) 13 *Harvard Human Rights Journal* 1–59.

(c) encourage ratification of the above-mentioned instruments or accession to those instruments, and to ensure their implementation;
(d) contribute to the reports which States are required to submit to United Nations bodies and committees, and to regional institutions, pursuant to their treaty obligations and, where necessary, to express an opinion on the subject, with due respect for their independence;
(e) cooperate with the United Nations and any other organization in the United Nations system, the regional institutions and the national institutions of other countries that are competent in the areas of the promotion and protection of human rights.[34]

While clearly the focus of an NHRI is going to be what happens in the country in which it is based, most NHRIs look to the international arena and aim to get involved, whether this is through the various UN forums, those conferences and events organised by NHRIsthemselves at an international or regional level, or regional human rights mechanisms, namely the UN Commission on Human Rights, UN treaty bodies, the AU and the African Commission on Human and Peoples' Rights. The founding legislation and document of NHRIs vary in the extent to which they recognise this role. For example, the Uganda Human Rights Commission Act 1997 provides that the Commission shall 'monitor the Government's compliance with international treaty and convention obligations on human rights.'[35] Other legislation has been less explicit and there has been criticism from some quarters that an NHRI should focus on doing work at home, rather than operating at the international level. In turn, however, NHRIs themselves have consistently stressed the importance of the international level for their work.

There are a number of reasons given by international bodies and by the NHRIs themselves as to why it is important for them to operate at both international and regional levels. As indicated by the Secretary General of the UN:

[32] See, eg Livingstone and Murray, above n 23; M Gomez, 'Sri Lanka's New Human Rights Commission' (1998) 20(2) *Human Rights Quarterly* 281–302; S Nfor Gwei, 'The Cameroon Experience in Creating and Running a National Commission for the Promotion and Protection of Human Rights', in K Hossain et al, *Human Rights Commissions and Ombudsman Offices. National Experiences Throughout the World* (Dordrecht, Kluwer Law International, 2001) 169–86; C Idike, 'Deflectionism or Activism? The Kenyan National Commission on Human Rights in Focus' (2004) 1(1) *Essex Human Rights Review* (2004) 40–53; C Norchi, 'The National Human Rights Commission of India as a Value-Creating Institution' in J Montgomery (ed), *Human Rights: Positive Policies in Asia and the Pacific Rim* (Hollis, New Hampshire, Hollis Publishing Company, 1998); A Whiting, 'Situating Suhakam. Human Rights Debates and Malaysia's National Human Rights Commission' (2002) 39 *Stanford Journal of International Law* 1.

[33] Eg J Hatchard, *Workshop on the Use of Public Inquiries and Formal Hearings by Commonwealth Human Rights Commissions*. Report. Organised by British Council and the Uganda Human Rights Commission, 25–27 February 2003.

[34] Paris Principles, para 3.

[35] Uganda Human Rights Commission Act 1997, 2 May 1997, s 8(1)(i); Constitution of the Republic of Uganda, Art 52(1)(h).

> NHRI are seen not only as institutions to which assistance may be provided, but also as partners that can provide important human rights knowledge and experience. NHRI are increasingly recognized by the international community as mechanisms that are essential to ensuring respect for the effective implementation of international human rights standards at the national level.[36]

As chapter 2 will illustrate, NHRIs can give an alternative voice to government before the international and regional monitoring bodies and are, therefore, another way of ensuring government accountability.[37] They can also ensure education and awareness-raising of international standards at the domestic level, as well as act as a bridge between NGOs and government at the international level, by bringing NGO concerns to international forums, by providing a forum at which NGOs and government can meet, and by feeding back issues from government to NGOs. As NHRIs at their regional and international meetings do not just focus on procedural issues, but discuss human rights from a thematic perspective, they can also assist in the development of international law. NHRIs have adopted statements leading up to international conferences and have recently played an important role in drafting of treaties. By meeting together, NHRIs offer collective support for each other's activities and share examples of good practice. Furthermore, NHRIs can ensure accountability and regulation of each other and, in turn, ensure the legitimacy and credibility of NHRIs through their procedures at the regional and international levels. Lastly, the international and regional forums in which NHRIs can participate offer them some protection for their work and NHRIs themselves are seen as another way in which other human rights defenders can be protected.

Despite these reasons for NHRIs having space to participate at the international and regional levels, there is an inconsistent approach to how their participation is determined and the extent of that involvement. As chapters 3 and 6 will illustrate, some of the UN organs have looked towards the accreditation procedure of NHRIs themselves to determine their participation in meetings, others, including the regional bodies, have been less prescriptive. Indeed, their participation may, in fact, depend on whether an NHRI is seen as part of the state, and thus part of its delegation, or as a non-state actor in its own right. As chapter 5 will discuss, although the role of non-state actors at the international and regional levels is relevant to NHRIs, these institutions do not fit easily into a state/non-state dichotomy.

[36] Effective Functioning of Human Rights Mechanisms, above n 4, at para 4.

[37] International Council on Human Rights Policy, *Performance and Legitimacy*, above n 31, at 99.

2

Legitimacy of NHRI Participation

IN DETERMINING THE extent of participation (National Human Rights Institutions) NHRIs should have at the international and regional levels, it is necessary to examine the reasons for their involvement. Just as many have examined the rationale and justification for permitting NGOs to participate at these levels, so similar arguments can be advanced with respect to NHRIs. On the one hand, they introduce a new perspective into international discussions.[1] On the other, it could also be argued that they offer expertise and neutrality, contacts and networks and can also assist in holding international institutions accountable.[2] Each of these will be examined in turn.

TO ENSURE GOVERNMENT ACCOUNTABILITY BY PROVIDING AN ALTERNATIVE VOICE TO GOVERNMENT

A common reason advanced by UN and African regional bodies and NHRIs themselves for their involvement at these levels is that they can provide another way of ensuring states' comply with their international obligations.[3] Indeed the National Institutions Unit (NI Unit) of the Office of the United Nations High Commissioner for Human Rights (OHCHR) sees them as playing 'a leading role' here.[4] They can do this in a number of ways, including, providing information to the international and regional bodies on the human rights situation in the country and acting as a filter for the international mechanism by educating those who may wish to use international procedures about the possibility of success in doing so, and in the process preventing the international bodies from being swamped by a flood of claims. They also have a wider educational function, by

[1] H Cullen and K Morrow, 'International Civil Society in International Law: The Growth of NGO Participation' (2001) 1 *Non-State Actors and International Law* 7–39, at 31.

[2] Ibid.

[3] National Institutions for the Promotion and Protection of Human Rights, Commission on Human Rights Resolution 1993/55, E/CN.4/RES/1993/55, 9 March 1993, preamble.

[4] 'Follow up activities have revealed that for countries that have received the trainings, national capacity to implement human rights treaty body recommendations has been strengthened through the enhancement of national protection measures with national human rights institutions playing a leading role', UN OHCHR, First Quarterly Public Report for 2005, National Institutions Activities, January–March 2005, March 2005, at 8. International Council on Human Rights Policy, *Performance and Legitimacy: National Human Rights Institutions* (Geneva, ICHRP, 2000) 99.

distributing materials of international and regional bodies at the domestic level.[5]

NHRIs can also check whether states have ratified certain treaties and encourage them to do so.[6] They have a number of other roles, from submitting reports on the situation in the country and making statements before international bodies alleging violations of human rights, to, in some instances, submitting cases under the communication procedures of international or regional treaties. They can also lobby international bodies to undertake certain action in respect of their home states and assist 'political and legislative bodies in the development of appropriate laws and practices,'[7] to ensure their compliance with international obligations.[8]

Particularly importantly is that the NHRI can be seen as the national mechanism through which it can be ensured that decisions and recommendations of international bodies are implemented. Some NHRIs have specific obligations in their founding legislation to monitor government compliance with international treaties.[9] In addition, the National Institutions Unit (NI Unit) of the Office of the United Nations High Commissioner for Human Rights (OHCHR) has been urged to send Concluding Observations from state reports[10] and decisions in

[5] General Recommendation XVII on the Establishment of National Institutions to Facilitate Implementation of the Convention, 25 March 1993. Resolution 58/175, National Institutions for the Promotion and Protection of Human Rights, 10 March 2004, para 9.

[6] Yaoundé Declaration, para 14. The fourth conference of African NHRIs, held in Kampala in August 2002, adopted the Kampala Declaration and called on African states to ratify ICESCR and put into place measures to protect such rights, ratify the Optional Protocol to the UN Convention on the Rights of the Child The Fourth Conference of African National Human Rights Institutions, Kampala, Uganda, 14–16 August 2002, Kampala Declaration, para 1(a)(vi), para 2(a)(v) respectively. 'This seems to be a useful and wholly proper function of a national institution,' International Council on Human Rights Policy, above n 3, at 100.

[7] Report of the UN High Commissioner for Human Rights to the Economic and Social Council, 29 June 2000, E/2000/83, para 79.

[8] The Copenhagen Declaration from the Sixth International Conference for National Institutions for the Promotion and Protection of Human Rights (Copenhagen and Lund, 10–13 April 2002), para 3(a) reads: 'working to ensure their respective governments ratify international human rights treaties, remove reservations contrary to the object and purpose of the treaty and ensure consistency between domestic laws, programmes and policies and international human rights standards.'

[9] Eg Uganda Human Rights Commission, see ch 1, n 35. However, it cannot deal with complaints which involve 'a matter involving the relations or dealings between the government and the government of any foreign state or international organisation,' Constitution of the Republic of Uganda, Art 53(4)(b). As long as it is not in this category, cases can be brought to the Commission based on rights in the Constitution as well as international human rights instruments to which Uganda is a signatory (Art 52(1)(h) of the Constitution of Uganda).

[10] The NI Unit of the OHCHR and the Treaty Body Recommendation Units provided training to some NHRIs on how to deal with Concluding Observations of treaties and a staff member at the OHCHR has been appointed in this respect, UN OHCHR, Member States Meeting Geneva, 28–29 June 2004. National Institutions Activities, January–June 2004, 16 June 2004, at 15. One workshop took place from 3–7 November 2003 (although no African NHRIs attended); another from 10–14 May 2004: Rwanda NHRI was included in this and they 'had the opportunity to participate in the sessions of the Committee Against Torture and the Committee on the Rights of the Child reviewing the report of their own country,' UN OHCHR, Member States Meeting Geneva, 28–29 June 2004. National Institutions Activities, January–June 2004, 16 June 2004, at 15. Similarly, at the end of the

individual communications to NHRIs to enable them to assist in implementation.[11] For example, one complainant, an NGO, noted the collaboration of the NHRI in Mauritania in implementing a decision granted in the NGO's favour by the African Commission[12] and NHRIs themselves have suggested that they could corroborate allegations of violations in cases before the African Commission.[13]

There have been some, albeit very few, instances where NHRIs have themselves taken cases to international or regional bodies under the communication procedures. The lack of cases may be due, in part, to the 'victim' requirement in many international treaties. However, where the admissibility requirements are more open, such as under the African Charter on Human and Peoples' Rights (ACHPR), there have been examples of NHRIs submitting cases on behalf of alleged victims of violations. Thus, in Communication 74/92, *Commission Nationale Des Droits de l'Homme et des Libertés v Chad*,[14] the NHRI alleged that serious or massive violations of the African Charter were taking place in the country. The African Commission during the course of considering the case heard from a representative from the NHRI and went on to find in its favour, holding there had been numerous violations of the African Charter.[15]

Furthermore, the African Commission has made it clear that if a case is submitted to the NHRI before being submitted to the Commission, it will not form part of domestic remedies procedure for the purpose of admissibility in Article 56 of the Charter. Thus, where the government of Nigeria in a case before the African Commission argued that the complainant had not put the issues before the Nigerian National Human Rights Commission prior to submitting the case to the African Commission, the latter held that although such an institution

examination of the state report of Congo in 2000, the Chair of the African Commission asked that NGOs and national institutions could monitor the situation in respect of responses sent by the state to the questions of the Commission.

[11] 'The Unit continued to systematically and promptly send to the national human rights institutions of the countries concerned Concluding Observations of treaty bodies and decisions under individual complains procedures,' UN OHCHR, First Quarterly Public Report, n 4, at 8. 'Increasingly, mandate-holders look to NIs to assist in ensuring that their recommendations are followed up at the national level. This is an important area of work for NIs and should be further encouraged,' Enhancing the Participation of National Human Rights Institutions in the Work of the Commission on Human Rights and its Subsidiary Bodies, Report of the Secretary General, 19 January 2005, E/CN.4/2005/107, para 26.

[12] See 30th session, comments from Institute for Human Rights and Development in Africa.

[13] Comments from the Nigerian National Human Rights Commission, 37th session of the African Commission.

[14] Ninth Annual Report of the African Commission on Human and Peoples' Rights, 1996, Annex VIII.

[15] Similarly, in Communication 135/94, *Kenya Human Rights Commission v Kenya*, the national institution of that country submitted a case relating to the ability of academic staff to register a trade union. The African Commission found the case inadmissible for non-exhaustion of domestic remedies, Ninth Annual Report, 1996, Annex VIII. The Follow-Up Committee on the Robben Island Guidelines has also encouraged NHRIs to bring cases to the African Commission on behalf of individuals on issues of torture, First meeting of the Follow Up Committee on Robben Island Guidelines, 19–20 February 2005, at 5–6.

granted remedies, and complainants should be encouraged to approach such bodies, it was still 'non-judicial' and therefore 'not part of the judicial structure of the state and the complainant was not obliged to seek a remedy from it.'[16] Despite this being a sensible approach, it has been argued that 'if one of the aims of national institutions is to relieve pressure on international mechanisms then complainants should certainly be encouraged to go through that process first.'[17]

NHRIs have therefore been seen as partners[18] of the international or regional bodies in assisting the latter to implement state obligations.[19] NHRIs themselves take this approach when making statements to the UN Commission on Human Rights and other bodies in providing information on the situation of human rights within their particular states, at the international level[20] and domestically.[21]

These various tasks can pose dilemmas for NHRIs and nowhere more so than with the involvement of NHRIs in the state reporting requirements under the UN treaties and the ACHPR. States are required to submit reports to the various treaty bodies on the measures they have taken at the domestic level to comply with their international obligations and these are usually required every few years[22] but the approach of UN treaty bodies and the African Commission is not consistent on the extent of NHRI involvement in the drafting and presentation

[16] Communication 268/2003, *Ilesanmi v Nigeria*, Eighteenth Annual Activity Report of the African Commission on Human and Peoples' Rights, 2004–2005, Annex III, EX.CL/199 (VII), para 42.

[17] International Council on Human Rights Policy, above n 4, at 100.

[18] Report of the United Nations High Commissioner for Human Rights and Follow up to the World Conference on Human Rights. *Effective Functioning of Human Rights Mechanisms, Note by the United Nations High Commissioner for Human Rights*, E/CN.4/2005/5, 5 July 2004, para 71. See also: Commission on Human Rights, *Effective Functioning of Human Rights Mechanisms: National Institutions and Regional Arrangements*, E/CN.4/2005/L.92/Rev.1, 19 April 2005: 'Welcomes greater efforts by the Office of the High Commissioner to engage national institutions as partners and provide them with opportunities to exchange experiences and best practices amongst themselves,' para 8.

[19] Report of the Secretary-General, Human Rights Questions: Human Rights Questions, including Alternative Approaches for Improving the Effective Enjoyment of Human Rights and Fundamental Freedoms, National Institutions for the Promotion and Protection of Human Rights, 20 September 1995, A/50/452, para 6(c).

[20] Eg in her statement to the 61st session of the UN Commission on Human Rights, the Chairperson of the Uganda Human Rights Commission noted the situation of human rights in her country and the difficulties the UHRC had faced in fulfilling its mandate, Statement from the Uganda Human Rights Commission, presented at the 61st Session of the UN Commission on Human Rights by Margaret Sekaggya, Chairperson, Uganda Human Rights Commission, April 2005, Geneva, www.nhri.net. A similar approach was taken by the Algerian Commission Nationale Consultative de Promotion et de Protection des Droits de l'Homme, Declaration de Maitre Mustpaha Farouk Ksentini President de la Commission Nationale Consultative de Promotion et de Protection des Droits de l'Homme, Geneve Avril 2005, www.nhri.net.

[21] In turn, the Uganda Human Rights Commission has noted whether the government has fulfilled its reporting obligations under international instruments. This referred to both UN treaties, ILO and ACHPR, see Uganda Human Rights Commission, Annual Report, at 41–42.

[22] Eg International Covenant on Civil and Political Rights, Art 40; International Covenant on Economic, Social and Cultural Rights, Art 16; African Charter on Human and Peoples' Rights, Art 62.

of the state report. The OHCHR has encouraged 'the involvement of national actors in the treaty reporting and implementation process, to enhance the participation of national institutions and civil society in the work of treaty bodies'[23] and some of the UN treaty bodies have simply asked that NHRIs submit shadow reports, in the same way as NGOs,[24] UN treaty bodies and the African Commission having relied on alternative sources of information (usually NGOs) when examining state reports.[25]

Other treaty bodies have gone further and required that the state should 'consult with independent national human rights institutions during the preparation of reports to the Committee' but with the caveat that 'states parties must respect the independence of these bodies and their independent role in providing information to the Committee. It is not appropriate to delegate to NHRIs the drafting of reports or to include them in the government delegation when reports are examined by the Committee.'[26]

In direct contrast to this, other treaty bodies have been less cautious and have encouraged NHRIs to participate in the drafting of the report and be part of the government delegation in the examination of that report. For example, in its General Recommendation on the Establishment of National Institutions to Facilitate Implementation of the Convention,[27] the Committee on the Elimination of Racial Discrimination recommended,

> that states parties establish national commissions or other appropriate bodies . . . to serve, inter alia, the following purposes: . . . to assist the government in the preparation of reports submitted to the Committee on ERD. Also recommends that where such commissions have been established, they should be associated with the preparation of reports and possibly included in government delegations in order to intensify the dialogue between the Committee and the state party concerned.[28]

[23] 'Strengthening the Implementation of Human Rights treaty recommendations through the enhancement of national protection measures,' Participation of the National Institutions Unit in the Treaty Body Recommendations Follow-Up Project, Annual Meeting of the ICC, April 2005, www.nhri.net.

[24] At the 37th session of the African Commission the Chair of the Commission in her opening speech said that NGOs and NHRIs should submit shadow reports to Article 62 reports. In the Report of the Retreat of Members of the African Commission on Human and Peoples' Rights (ACHPR) facilitated by the Office of the High Commissioner for Human Rights (OHCHR), African Union Conference Centre, Addis Ababa, Ethiopia, 24–26 September 2003, it was noted that in attendance was the chair of the Coordinating Committee of African National Human Rights Institutions among others. This noted that shadow reports to Art 62 reports from NHRIs as well as NGOs were useful sources of information and that NHRIs in particular 'should be encouraged to prepare and submit Shadow reports,' at 3. Similarly, see NI Unit, *The United Nations Treaty Bodies and National Institutions*, http://www.nhri.net/pdf/TBs_and_NIs.pdf, at 2.

[25] G Rubagotti, 'Non-Governmental Organisations and the Reporting Obligation under the International Covenant on Civil and Political Rights' (2005) 5 *Non-State Actors and International Law* 59–75, at 66.

[26] General Comment No 2, The Role of Independent National Human Rights Institutions in the Promotion and Protection of the Rights of the Child, 31st session, 2002, HRI/GEN/1/Rev.7, para 21.

[27] General Recommendation XVII, above n 5.

[28] Ibid, paras 1 and 2.

The NI Unit suggests something further still, noting that the involvement of the NHRI may be particularly useful when 'there is a lack of institutional capacity within state party administrations,' but this should not compromise the independence of the institution and 'may only occur until such time as the government is able to take full control of its responsibilities.'[29]

The present situation clearly does not present a coherent and consistent approach to the position of NHRIs in the state reporting mechanism and is, arguably, a 'dangerous blurring of roles.'[30] This is confused further in the draft Harmonized Guidelines on Reporting under the International Human Rights Treaties, including Guidelines on a Common Core Document and Treaty-Specific Targeted Documents,[31] which do not provide any express statement that NHRIs should be involved in the drafting of state party reports. However, as part of the content of the common core document, states are required to comment on the process by which reports are prepared, including, 'independent participation, where appropriate, of National Human Rights Institutions constituted in accordance with the Paris Principles in the reporting process, in monitoring government reports to the treaty bodies and in actively monitoring the implementation of concluding observations/comments of treaty bodies at the national level,'[32] as well as to include information on whether there are any national institutions to oversee implementation of human rights, what the mandate of such institutions is and what resources are available to them.[33]

It is unsurprising, given this ambiguity, that NHRIs themselves have expressed discomfort with their ambiguous role in state reporting. As the Malawi Human Rights Commission noted at the 17th session of the NHRIs' International Co-ordinating Committee, it was not entirely sure how to handle requests from treaty bodies to participate in the state reporting process. The state report of Malawi was due to be examined under CEDAW and the CEDAW Committee had requested the NHRI to say something on their role regarding implementation of CEDAW in the country. However, as the delegate from the Malawian Commission stated to the 17th session: 'we are in a fix in terms of what exactly should happen. As when we were meeting with government delegation to say we were independent, the government said we should be part of their delegation.'[34]

[29] National Institutions Unit, above n 24, at 2.

[30] International Council on Human Rights Policy, above n 4, at 100.

[31] 1 June 2005, HRI/MC/2005/3.

[32] Draft Harmonized Guidelines on Reporting under the International Human Rights Treaties, including Guidelines on a Common Core Document and Treaty-Specific Targeted Documents, 1 June 2005, HRI/MC/2005/3, para 50(b).

[33] Ibid, para 47(f). States are also expressly required to provide information on 'any institutions created for the protection and promotion of human rights at the national level, including those with specific responsibilities with regard to gender equality, race relations and children's rights, their precise mandate, composition, financial resources and activities, and whether such institutions are regarded as independent in accordance with the . . . Paris Principles,' para 48(b).

[34] 17th session of the ICC, April 2006, notes on file with author.

A more sensible approach is advocated by Brice Dickson, former Chief Commissioner of the Northern Ireland Human Rights Commission:

> It is much preferable, in my view, if NHRIs do not identify themselves too closely with the periodic reports submitted to the treaty-monitoring bodies because when the bodies are examining the state representatives it is useful for them to have the independent view of the national institution to fall back on. My own Commission likes to get sight of drafts of the UK government's periodic reports so that we can suggest improvements to them . . . but we also like to produce our own 'shadow' reports which we send separately to the treaty-monitoring body to assist it in formulating questions for state representatives.[35]

Potentially even more problematic is where the NHRI itself is a central feature of the state's international obligation. The Optional Protocol to the UN Convention Against Torture (OPCAT),[36] under Article 18, requires that states 'maintain, designate or establish one or more national preventive mechanisms for the prevention of torture at the domestic level. Mechanisms established by decentralized units may be designated as national preventive mechanisms for the purposes of the present Protocol if they are in conformity with its provisions.' A sub-committee is also established at the international level to visit places where persons are deprived of their liberty, and to advise states on the establishment of their national preventive mechanisms, advise and maintain contact with the national mechanisms themselves, make necessary recommendations, and co-operate with relevant international and regional organisations.[37] A significant number of states have appointed, or are considering appointing, their NHRI to undertake this role and, as the NI Unit of the OHCHR has stated, 'it is clear that OPCAT is complementary to the already existing role of many NHRIs. It can empower NHRIs, should the state party determined that they will be the national protection mechanism under the Protocol, to ensure that they are adequately resourced to undertake the tasks and to also have their staff properly trained in this area.'[38] Indeed the Paris Principles are being taken as the standards against which such institutions should be examined.[39]

In these situations the NHRI itself is part of the state apparatus being evaluated under the Optional Protocol commitments that it has assumed. This raises potential difficulties in determining who is responsible. Fortunately, the Optional Protocol gets around this by providing for the sub-committee to oversee the performance of the national mechanisms, through dialogue directly with

[35] Brice Dickson, Chief Commissioner, Northern Ireland Human Rights Commission, Address to the Workshop on the Paris Principles, Tirana, Albania, 5 May 2004, www.nihrc.org

[36] Optional Protocol to the Convention against Torture and Other Cruel, Inhuman or Degrading Treatment or Punishment (OPCAT), Resolution 57/199, 9 January 2003.

[37] Art 11 OPCAT.

[38] NI Unit, above n 24, at 4.

[39] Art 18(4) OPCAT.

them as well as with the states.[40] This avoids potential difficulties where, for example, a government establishes a national mechanism, which may be the NHRI itself, that complies with the Paris Principles but which, in its performance, does not fulfil its expectations. The sub-committee can enter into discussions and direct recommendations at the national institution itself. On the one hand, the manner in which it functions falls under the state's treaty obligations and it is indirectly responsible for it. On the other, this raises difficult questions in trying to protect the independence of the institution. The international bodies monitoring compliance with the Optional Protocol and other provisions will have to carefully consider the various responsibilities of the actors at play.

AS EXPERTS

Just as the contribution of NGOs at the international and regional levels is seen as important because they provide a level of expertise on human rights, so NHRIs could argue the same.[41] As the Human Rights Commissioner for Malawi at the UN Human Rights Commission's 61st session stated: 'NHRI's possess a lot of information and technical expertise on the human rights situations in their respective countries that the UN Commission can benefit from when coming up with its Country Reports on human rights.'[42] NHRIs are in a useful position as not only do they potentially have expertise in human rights generally, but they have knowledge of the particular state, thereby being invited 'to submit regular written reports on human rights situations in Africa in such a manner as would assist the Commission in the execution of its mandate.'[43] Many international and regional bodies have seen the contribution of NHRIs as an additional necessary element in providing a further check on what is being espoused by the state on the one hand and NGOs on the other.

Furthermore, international and regional bodies have involved NHRIs in the development of international human rights norms and standards. This has included their participation on working groups, for example, the African Commission's Follow Up Committee on the Robben Island Guidelines relating

[40] Eg Art 16 of the Optional Protocol provides that 'The Subcommittee on Prevention shall communicate its recommendations and observations confidentially to the State Party and, if relevant, to the national preventive mechanism.'

[41] 'Here the issue is not the legitimacy of a claim to obedience, but rather the legitimacy of participation of nongovernmental, non-commercial actors in distinct roles in the international governance process,' and that it is not necessary for them to be representative but they can be experts or sources of information, ML Schweitz, 'NGO Participation in International Governance: The Question of Legitimacy' (1995) 89 *American Society of International Law Proceedings* 415–20, at 419.

[42] Statement by Justice Elton Singini, SC, Law Commissioner/Human Rights Commissioner for Malawi to the 61st Session of the United Nations Commission on Human Rights, Geneva, Switzerland, April 2005, at 2.

[43] Resolution on the Human Rights Situation in Africa, 13th Annual Report of the ACHPR, Annex IV.

to torture.[44] Included in the outcomes of meetings held by NHRIs themselves are discussions on thematic issues with, in some cases, development of standards. The Declaration from the fifth African NHRI conference in Abuja November 2005 focused on economic, social and cultural rights, recognising the importance for human developments of various economic, social and cultural rights.[45] NHRIs are contributing to development of legal standards[46] with the adoption of documents such as the New Delhi Concluding Statement, and a Montreal Declaration on Economic, Social and Cultural Rights,[47] and helping to elaborate standards on racism and racial discrimination,[48] migration,[49] gender,[50] indigenous peoples,[51] minorities, HIV/AIDS,[52] conflict prevention and torture,[53] and rights of the child.[54] Their participation in international and regional conferences, such as the Durban World Conference on Racism in

[44] Which has a member of the Senegalese Human Rights Commission in its composition, Mr Malick Sow.

[45] Fifth Conference of African National Human Rights Institutions, Abuja, 8–10 November 2005, Abuja Declaration.

[46] Further, the fourth conference of African NHRIs, held in Kampala in August 2002, adopted the Kampala Declaration: 'request the office of the High Commissioner for Human Rights in conjunction with UNESCO to spearhead efforts towards the creation of a Convention on the Right to peace,' The Fourth Conference of African National Human Rights Institutions. Held in Kampala Uganda, 14–16 August 2002, Kampala Declaration, para 2(c)(i) and (ii). See also: Regional Conference on the Human Rights Dimensions of Corruption, the Nairobi Declaration, March 2006, on file with author.

[47] Eg International Round table on NHRIs and the Implementation of Economic, Social and Cultural Rights, 29 November–1 December 2005, 'to strengthen the capacity of NHRIs to address economic, social and cultural rights and to advance knowledge on the international human rights instruments and the principles that guide state responsibilities in relation to ESCR,' Effective Functioning of Human Rights Mechanisms: National Institutions and Regional Arrangements. National Institutions for the Promotion and Protection of Human Rights. Report of the Secretary-General, E/CN.4/2006/101, 24 January 2006, para 75. The Montreal Declaration was the outcome of the first congress of the Association Francophone des Commissions Nationales des Droits de l'Homme on Economic, Social and Cultural Rights, 29 September–1 October 2005, Effective Functioning of Human Rights Mechanisms, ibid, at para 77. See also African Commission on Human and Peoples' Rights, Resolution on Economic, Social and Cultural Rights in Africa, ACHPR/Res.73 (XXXVI)/04.

[48] Effective Functioning of Human Rights Mechanisms, ibid, at para 80. Eg CCANI should recommend strategies for its members on racial discrimination. Its is also recommended that states set up NHRIs, and a regional anti-discrimination network be set up composed of NHRIs among others, Implementation of the Durban Programme of Action: An Exchange of Ideas on how to move Forward. Seminar of Experts for the African Region, organised by the Office of the High Commissioner for Human Rights in Co-operation with the United Nations Office in Nairobi (UNON), 16–18 September 2002, http://www.nhri.net/pdf/Nairobi-Recommendations.pdf, paras A.1.C and 4.D. Re participation of NHRIs in the World Conference Against Racism, see: Rules of Procedure of World Conference, Rule 65, A/CONF.189/92.

[49] The ICC concentrated on this issue at its 16th session in April 2005, Effective Functioning of Human Rights Mechanisms, n 47, at para 81.

[50] Ibid, para 82.

[51] Ibid, paras 86–87.

[52] Ibid, para 89.

[53] Ibid, paras 90–93.

[54] Ibid, para 94.

September 2001,[55] and celebrations such as the fiftieth anniversary of the Universal Declaration of Human Rights (UDHR),[56] has enabled them to make collective statements and input into the resulting declarations.

Certainly, the participation of NHRIs does not necessarily mean that their role is enhanced more in the final texts adopted,[57] but in some instances NHRI participation can influence the content of the resulting documents. As is illustrated in chapter 3, there is considerable scope now, and the opportunity to participate in relevant meetings and debates, surrounding the reform of the UN human rights system, for NHRIs to become a more visible presence in the procedures and to reflect this in the documentation adopted.[58] Furthermore, for the first time, NHRIs have been allowed to participate in the drafting of a UN treaty, the International Convention on the Rights and Dignity of Persons with Disabilities[59] and chosen to play an active role in its ad hoc committee.[60] This

[55] Eg, see Statement by National Human Rights Commission, Nigeria, at the Conference Against Racism, Racial Discrimination, Xenophobia and Related Intolerance, Durban South Africa, 31 August–7 September 2001, www.un.org/WCAR/statements/hr_com_nigeriaE.htm; Statement at the Plenary by Dr Barney Pityana, Designated Spokesperson. Joint Statement of National Institutions, 4 September 2001, www.unhchr.ch. See also the result of regional discussions leading up to the World Conference, Third Conference of African National Human Rights Institutions Held in Lomé, Togo, 14–16 March 2001, Lomé Declaration, para VII.4; Report of the Regional Conference for Africa, Dakar, 22–24 January 2001, Reports of preparatory meetings and Activities at the International, Regional and National Levels, World Conference against Racism, Racial Discrimination, Xenophobia and Related Intolerance, 27 March 2001, A/CONF.189/PC.2/8, at preamble.

[56] Where NHRIs were called on by the General Assembly to play 'an active role in the celebrations marking the 50th anniversary of the Universal Declaration of Human Rights at the national and local levels,' Resolution 52/128, National Institutions for the Promotion and Protection of Human Rights, 26 February 1998, para 8.

[57] Report of the Regional Conference for Africa, Dakar, 22–24 January 2001, Reports of preparatory meetings and Activities at the International, Regional and National Levels, World Conference against Racism, Racial Discrimination, Xenophobia and Related Intolerance, 27 March 2001, A/CONF.189/PC.2/8, at Appendix I, List of Attendance.

[58] Statement by Morten Kjaerum, Director, Danish Institute for Human Rights. Chairperson International Coordinating Committee of National Institutions for the Promotion and Protection of Human Rights (ICC), at the Sixty-First Session of the Commission on Human Rights, Geneva, 13 April 2005, at 1.

[59] The General Assembly invited NHRIs to participate in drafting a Comprehensive and Integral International Convention on the Protection and Promotion of the Rights and Dignity of Persons with Disabilities (Resolution 57/229), Enhancing the Participation of National Human Rights Institutions in the Work of the Commission on Human Rights and its Subsidiary Bodies, above n 11.

[60] The African Union's Economic, Social and Cultural Council (ECOSOC) in its decision 2004/14, Comprehensive and Integral International Convention on Protection and Promotion of the Rights and Dignity of Persons with Disabilities, 'invites . . . human rights institutions and independent experts with an interest in the matter, to continue to make available to the Ad Hoc Committee suggestions about elements to be considered in a draft international convention.' African NHRIS should also 'fully participate in the upcoming discussions on the Draft Convention for the Protection and Promotion of the Rights and Dignity of Persons with Disabilities and as much as possible to assist representatives of Persons with Disabilities to participate in discussions.' On this latter point it 'requests the Office of the High Commissioner for Human Rights to assist and facilitate a meeting of African NHRIs to discuss issues related to the Promotion and Protection of Rights of Persons with Disabilities in preparation for the 2003 Geneva meeting on the draft Convention on the Promotion and Protection of the Rights and Dignity of Persons with Disabilities,' The Fourth Conference of African National Human Rights Institutions. Held in Kampala Uganda, 14–16 August 2002, Kampala Declaration, paras 4(b)(iii) and 4(c)(i).

precedent has been followed with the involvement of NHRIs in the working group considering an optional protocol to the International Covenant on Economic, Social and Cultural Rights.[61]

The difficulty, however, is that the basis on which NHRIs may be invited to participate in the development of international human rights standards, namely their expertise, may be flawed. Although the NHRI may be familiar with the situation in the particular state, not all members of NHRIs are 'experts' in human rights, some having only received minimum training and many not requiring human rights knowledge as a criterion for membership. Added to this, the fact that some NHRIs may simply be no more than another spokesperson for government, the legitimacy of their involvement in drafting international and regional documents is questionable.

AS A COLLECTIVE VOICE FOR NHRIs

A further justification for NHRI participation in international and regional arenas is that it 'recognises the need to bring the collective voice of Africa to promote an effective use of African human rights instruments for the enforcement of human rights.'[62] Indeed, the conferences held among NHRIs themselves have been created for this very purpose, among others, for example, the Chairperson of the Coordinating Committee of African National Human Rights Institutions (CCANI) 'is the spokesperson for African NHRIs at all levels and shall represent the Committee whether the interests of African NHRIs require.'[63] Clearly the International Coordinating Committee of National Human Rights Institutions (ICC) is also seen as carrying out this function and there have been attempts by NHRIs, albeit not very successfully, to meet prior to the African Commission on Human and Peoples' Rights in order to present a collective view to the Commission.[64]

TO PROTECT HUMAN RIGHTS DEFENDERS

The concept of a 'human rights defender' is usually equated with a representative of an NGO.[65] Indeed, those working on standards for the protection of human rights defenders have stressed the role that NHRIs can play in the

[61] OHCHR, An Optional Protocol to the International Covenant on Economic, Social and Cultural Rights. Note for National Human Rights Institutions, 2006, on file with author.

[62] Durban Declaration from the 2nd African NHRI conference, held from 1–3 July 1998, preamble.

[63] Rules of Procedure of the Coordinating Committee of African National Institutions for the Promotion and Protection of Human Rights, Art 17(b).

[64] Eg as at the 30th session of the African Commission.

[65] Declaration on the Right and Responsibilities of Individuals, Groups, and Organs of Society to Promote and Protect Universally Recognized Human Rights and Fundamental Freedoms, UN GA 1999, GA Res.53/144 (1999).

protection of these defenders. Thus, the UN Declaration on Human Rights Defenders provides specifically that 'the state shall ensure and support, where appropriate, the creation and development of further independent national institutions for the promotion and protection of human rights and fundamental freedoms in all territory under its jurisdiction, whether they be ombudsmen, human rights commissions or any other form of national institution.'[66] Similarly, in her reports to particular states, the Special Representative of the Secretary-General on the Situation of Human Rights Defenders, Hina Jilani, has often approached the NHRI as being a part of the state which should protect defenders of human rights.[67] The African Commission has followed a similar line in its Resolution on the Protection of Human Rights Defenders of the African Commission which called on its Special Rapporteur on Human Rights Defenders 'to cooperate and engage in dialogue with Member States, National Human Rights Institutions, relevant intergovernmental bodies, international and regional mechanisms of protection of human rights defenders, human rights defenders and other stake holders.'[68]

Yet the definition of a human rights defender is clearly broad enough to encompass NHRIs, but the perception that members of the NHRIs themselves as deserving of protection has received less attention.[69] This is something NHRIs have seen as important, as reflected in the adoption of some guidance on early warning mechanisms for NHRIs.[70] These look at the fact that members of NHRIs are often subject to threats, whether towards their abolition, from financial, restricting mandate, or to their staff and members themselves. The NHRIs International Coordinating Committee is therefore deemed, although not

[66] Art 14(3).

[67] Eg 'such a widespread perception of insecurity among defenders implies that protection mechanisms, such as the NHRC . . . are not adequately supporting and protecting defenders,' Mission to Thailand, Report Submitted by the Special Representative of the Secretary General on the Situation of Human Rights Defenders, Hina Jilani, E/CN.4/2004/94/Add.1, 12 March 2004, at para 71. In addition, talking about Latin America, 'despite an increasing trend by governments in the region to set up human rights institutions and initiatives, a lack of political and financial support has rendered these institutions ineffective in protecting human rights. Poor coordination of such mechanisms results in a failure to determine responsibility and prevents any consolidated action. Confronting this situation implies a substantial depletion of resources for human rights activists,' Report of the Special Representative of the Secretary General on Human Rights Defenders, A/57/182, 2 July 2002, para 40. Furthermore, 'even where national human rights institutions such as commissions and ombudsmen exist, defenders have received little relief . . . This indicates that in a number of these countries institutions are weak and lack independence and credibility,' para 89.

[68] Resolution on the Protection of Human Rights Defenders, above n 66, at para 1(c).

[69] Although there has been some recognition of this by the UN Special Representative of the Secretary- General on the Situation of Human Rights Defenders, who has criticised states for not giving adequate powers or independence to NHRIs, and also where members of NHRI who have criticised governments have been threatened, eg Mission to Thailand, Report Submitted by the Special Representative of the Secretary General on the Situation of Human Rights Defenders, above n 68, at paras 11–13. 'The NHRC's objectives make it an important part of the national human rights protection system. Strengthened resources and greater respect for its independence and response to its concerns would improve its efficacy, strengthen human rights protection and increase its capacity to support defenders,' para 13.

[70] National Institutions in Need: Guidelines for Early Warning, on file with author.

expressly, but impliedly, to have the mandate to 'take action in support of its members when under threat, . . . by virtue of its mandate to strengthen NIs and to ensure that they conform to the Paris Principles; to coordinate joint activities and cooperation among NIs; and to liaise with the United Nations and other international organizations.' The action envisaged relies on consideration of a number of factors including whether there is (1) sufficient evidence to justify a particular course of action; (2) whether the institution is actually an NHRI and (3) what will be the most effective way of intervening.

The NHRI itself can contact the chair of the ICC, the Regional Coordinator and the OHCHR, and any action taken must be done with the consent of the NHRI itself. Steps these bodies could take include posting information on the www.nhri.net website; requesting the chair of the ICC and OHCHR 'to write or make contact with the requisite authority concerning the alleged threat; ICC Chair can request the intervention of other NIs and in particular ICC Members; OHCHR can, if appropriate, make contact with the governmental authorities.' Additional pressure can, if necessary, be applied and includes using the media, requesting intervention of UN organs such as Special Rapporteurs or UN treaty bodies, and informing international NGOs or the UN Commission on Human Rights under agenda item 18(b). Several NHRIs have in fact already requested assistance from the ICC under this mechanism, alleging 'external pressure on the work of the National Human Rights Commission' of Kenya; 'reports of lack of appointments to, and staff in, the National Human Rights Commission of Madagascar,' and 'reports of alleged discrepancy between legal framework and appointment procedures applied for members of the Commission Nationale des Droits de l'Homme et des Libertés Fondamentales' of Niger.[71] The ICC has not been clear in its approach as to how to deal with these instances and has suggested that they have implications for accreditation and review processes.[72]

OTHER REASONS FOR NHRI PARTICIPATION

UN bodies and the African Commission on Human and Peoples' Rights have encouraged the participation of NHRIs in their work because these institutions offer another avenue by which their recommendations and concerns can be taken directly to the state[73] and thereby 'act as a channel between action at the international level-through international treaty bodies, the special procedures, human rights resolutions and other mechanisms-and action at the national level.'[74]

[71] ICC, Draft Report on ICC Activities 2005–2006, 17th Session of the International Coordinating Committee of NHRIs, 10–11 April 2006, on file with author, para 1.3.

[72] See ch 6.

[73] Report of the UN High Commissioner for Human Rights to the Economic and Social Council, 29 June 2000, E/2000/83, para 78.

[74] The Copenhagen Declaration from the Sixth International Conference for National Institutions for the Promotion and Protection of Human Rights (Copenhagen and Lund, 10–13 April 2002), para 2a.

Similarly, NHRIs can act as a bridge between NGOs and government, on the one hand,[75] and NGOs and the international and regional bodies on the other. As one Commissioner stated at the 30th session of the African Commission,

> close links with national institutions and NGOs, not only within that country but also internationally, is a very important aspect of the work of the national institutions because they can give support to the work of the NGOs and work in collaboration with them and NGOs can also strengthen work by national institutions and all this can be done in an atmosphere of dialogue and respect of competence of institutions and NGOs.[76]

CONCLUSION

Despite the variety of laudable reasons for the involvement of NHRIs in UN and African Commission sessions, it is worth questioning the validity of some of them. They are not necessarily experts. Neither can they claim, as some NGOs may, legitimacy by being non-governmental,[77] or by being representative of a particular interest or group.[78] Attention then falls on the extent to which the NHRI is independent. Yet this raises inherent tensions.

Governments can also use NHRIs to enhance their reputation at the international and national level. There is evidence of this occurring, with some NHRIs using their platform at the international and regional levels to criticise NGOs. For example, at the 30th session of the African Commission, the representative of the Commission in Rwanda was concerned that international NGOs made comments without objectivity and some of their allegations were baseless, such as their statements that national institutions were a masquerade and voices of government.[79]

[75] OC Okafor and SC Agbakwa, 'On Legalism, Popular Agency and "Voices of Suffering": The Nigerian National Human Rights Commission in Context,' (2002) 24 *Human Rights Quarterly* 662–720.

[76] Report of the 30th session of the African Commission, on file with author. See Okafor and Agbakwa, ibid.

[77] Cullen and Morrow, above n 1.

[78] 'Civil organisations such as NGOs are assumed to give a voice to stakeholders and issues that are otherwise excluded from politics and political forums. Provided that an NGO is recognised as a legitimate information provider and issue advocate, this role can generate a political legitimacy and an acceptance to speak for and formally represent affected groups in official settings,' D Berlin, 'The Key to Green Power–Explaining NGO Influence in Global Environmental Governance Structure,' prepared for NISA-NOPSA Conference, Reykjavik, 11–13 August 2005, Workshop Globalization as Individualization and Destabilization, at 16. Many contest whether NGOs are in fact representative of those whose interests they seek to project. See, for example, D Chandler, 'The Road to Military Humanitarianism: How the Human Rights NGOs Shaped A New Humanitarian Agenda' (2001) 23 *Human Rights Quarterly* 678–700; A de Waal, 'Human Rights in Africa: Values, Institutions and Opportunities' in K Hossain et al, *Human Rights Commissions and Ombudsman Offices. National Experiences Throughout the World* (Dordrecht, Kluwer Law International, 2001) 759–81; OC Okafor, 'Reconceiving "Third World" Legitimate Governance Struggles in our Time: Emergent Imperatives for Rights Activism' (2000) 6 *Buffalo Human Rights Law Review* 1.

[79] See also similar comments made at the UN Human Rights Commission's 61st session, see ch 5.

One outcome may be, as Cardenas notes, that in 'co-opting' human rights groups,

> there is a danger that the state will move to displace non-state actors. This would explain why national governments might agree to create institutions that monitor the very international norms they violate. Likewise, as NHRIs acquire more formal international powers, they may begin to compete directly with nongovernmental groups for resources as mundane but as important as speaking time in international forums. Domestically, NHRIs could help states occupy the "space" now filled by societal groups, thereby controlling the human rights agenda and silencing calls for accountability.[80]

Despite this, the UN, AU and African Commission on Human and Peoples' Rights, as well as NHRIs themselves, have not really examined why NHRIs should be involved at this level, preferring to concentrate, as chapters 3 and 4 explain, on the practicalities of how, and how much, they should participate. Yet until the validity of their participation is properly justified the approach is likely to continue to be inconsistent.

[80] S Cardenas, 'Emerging Global Actors: The United Nations and National Human Rights Institutions' (2003) 9 *Global Governance* 23–42, at 37.

3

The Role of NHRIs in the United Nations

DESPITE NHRIs BEING created at the national level and therefore domestic institutions, encouragement for their creation and support for their strengthening, as well as the standards by which they have come to be evaluated, have been very much linked to the UN and the latter's involvement in their development.[1] Indeed, there is evidence that encouragement by the UN has led to an increase in these types of institutions being established.[2] Arguably states have not been uncomfortable with UN involvement as this has enabled them to create institutions that could act as a buffer to further encroachment on their domestic sovereignty.[3] The UN has thus paid NHRIs increased attention since the 1970s, with the move towards standard setting in the 1990s and the adoption of the Paris Principles.[4] Support towards NHRIs now includes creating links between NHRIs, although only really since the 1990s; supporting international and regional workshops on NHRIs, and capacity building, namely giving governments support and assistance in establishing such bodies, without which the establishment of some might not have been possible.[5] Yet it has been criticised for focusing too much on encouraging states to set up such institutions, without sufficient regard for their effectiveness. As Human Rights Watch noted:

The Office of the High Commissioner for Human Rights appears to have fully embraced the premise that the effective enjoyment of human rights calls for the establishment of a national human rights institution and is actively marketing human rights commissions. This presumes that the creation of a human rights commission will, in itself, contribute to the promotion and protection of human rights, an unfounded premise as this report shows. There has been no serious effort to question this premise in internal evaluations nor does

[1] Cardenas argues that the UN 'has played a crucial role in creating and strengthening NHRIs. It has done so by means of four mechanisms: standard setting, capacity building, network facilitating, and membership granting,' S Cardenas, 'Emerging Global Actors: The United Nations and National Human Rights Institutions' (2003) 9 *Global Governance* 23–42, at 24.

[2] Ibid, at 35.

[3] Ibid, at 29.

[4] Ibid, at 29–30.

[5] Ibid, at 31.

there appear to have been any serious policy discussions, based on the record of existing national human rights institutions, to take stock and question whether this policy direction should expand, or even continue.[6]

In the process of all this involvement it is the UN that has helped define the very concept of the NHRI.[7] As to how NHRI are treated at the UN, the UN Charter mechanism and the UN treaty bodies have taken slightly different perspectives.

UN HUMAN RIGHTS COMMISSION AND SUBSIDIARY BODIES AND THE INTERNATIONAL COORDINATING COMMITTEE OF NATIONAL HUMAN RIGHTS INSTITUTIONS (ICC)

Over the years the UN Human Rights Commission and its subsidiary bodies have shown considerable inconsistency in their treatment of NHRIs. Early treatment saw them as little more than supporting the work of the UN Commission on Human Rights, rather than as independent bodies in their own right.[8] Culminating with the adoption of the Paris Principles in 1993,[9] they dealt with NHRIs through two separate procedures[10]: the technical assistance programme and the Special Advisor on NHRIs in the Office of the High Commissioner of Human Rights, the latter created in 1995. In addition, the United Nations Development Programme (UNDP) played a role in providing financial and other support to these institutions. Initially, however, despite a memorandum of understanding being signed,[11] there was little integration between the Office of the United Nations High Commissioner for Human Rights (OHCHR) and the UNDP.

On the one hand, the Special Advisor gained a huge amount of expertise but lacked information on the specific countries: 'As a result, the advice given may be generic and tied to the Paris Principles, rather than based on an in-depth understanding of what might work best in the political and cultural context of a specific country.'[12] In response to such concerns, the OHCHR moved to establish a National Institutions Unit to co-ordinate activities not only with respect to the UN Human Rights Commission and ICC, but across treaty bodies and elsewhere. This National Institutions Unit (NI Unit) within the OHCHR provides advisory services, such as giving training on how to create NHRIs or

[6] Human Rights Watch, *Protectors or Pretenders? Government Human Rights Commissions in Africa* (New York, Human Rights Watch, 2001) 73.

[7] Cardenas, above n 1, at 35.

[8] Ibid, at 28.

[9] National Institutions for the Promotion and Protection of Human Rights, General Assembly Resolution 48/134 of 20 December 1993, A/RES/48/134, 4 March 1994.

[10] Human Rights Watch, above n 6, at 73.

[11] Ibid, at 75.

[12] Ibid, 74–75.

strengthen them where they already exist.[13] It also assists NHRI participation in UN Charter and treaty bodies[14] and acts as secretariat to the ICC.

The extent to which NHRIs could participate in the UN meetings and forums has not been consistent. On the one hand, it has been suggested that NHRIs are 'granted the same status as the specialised agencies and space should be made available to them so that their representatives could express their views as representatives of independent bodies.'[15] On other occasions they have been treated as NGOs,[16] and yet on others as part of government delegations.[17] In 1999 NHRIs were given a special section at the Commission on Human Rights by the chair and it was decided that they should have a separate nameplate, 'national institutions' on the floor.[18] This practice was continued in subsequent sessions of the UN Commission.[19]

In more recent years, participation in the UN Commission on Human Rights and its subsidiary bodies[20] under the UN Charter mechanisms has taken increasing account of accreditation by the International Coordinating Committee (ICC) of NHRIs. As the ICC is composed of NHRIs themselves, the UN

[13] See, eg Effective Functioning of Human Rights Mechanisms: National Institutions and Regional Arrangements. National Institutions for the Promotion and Protection of Human Rights, Report of the Secretary General, 24 January 2006, E/CN.4/2006/101, at paras 5–6.

[14] Ibid.

[15] Report of the Secretary-General, Human Rights Questions: Human Rights Questions, including Alternative Approaches for Improving the Effective Enjoyment of Human Rights and Fundamental Freedoms, National Institutions for the Promotion and Protection of Human Rights, 20 September 1995, A/50/452. The report also noted what status NHRIs should be given within the UN: In his reply '. . . the Secretary General said he believed that the question of the status of national institutions at the meetings of the United Nations human rights bodies was a matter for the Commission on Human Rights and the Economic and Social Council to decide and that he expected them to reach an appropriate decision,' paras 36–37.

[16] As regards the UN Commission's sub-bodies, participation in the Sub-Commission on Human Rights, from its 55th session in 2004, NHRIs have been present on the same basis as NGOs, namely, one statement per each item, of 7 minutes maximum. The January 2005 report of the Secretary-General notes that very few NHIRS have used this opportunity, mainly because of lack of financial means, Enhancing the Participation of National Human Rights Institutions in the Work of the Commission on Human Rights and its Subsidiary Bodies, Report of the Secretary General, 19 January 2005, E/CN.4/2005/107, para 24.

[17] Paper of the Australian EOC to the 9th Annual Meeting of Asia Pacific Forum on NHRIs on 'The Role of NIs in the United Nations Commission on the Status of Women.' As the January 2005 report of the Secretary-General notes, 'at present, NIs do not have standing in their own right in the Commission on the Status of Women, thus making it necessary for NIs to participate in its sessions as part of their government's delegation,' Enhancing the Participation of National Human Rights Institutions in the Work of the Commission on Human Rights and its Subsidiary Bodies, ibid, at para 17.

[18] Resolution 1999/72, para 15.

[19] Resolutions 2000/76, 2001/80, 2002/83, 2003/76 and 2004/75 which refer to sessions after this when NHRIs were able to participate in the UN Human Rights Commission, Enhancing the Participation of National Human Rights Institutions in the Work of the Commission on Human Rights and its Subsidiary Bodies, above n 16.

[20] The Secretary-General's Report recommends accreditation to speak at Sub-Commission meetings should be the same as for the Human Rights Commission, Enhancing the Participation of National Human Rights Institutions in the Work of the Commission on Human Rights and its Subsidiary Bodies, above n 16, at para 24.

Commission on Human Rights has therefore relied on a form of self-regulation as a key element in determining the extent of their participation.

THE INTERNATIONAL COORDINATING COMMITTEE OF NHRIs (ICC)

At its second international workshop bringing together NHRIs from across the world,[21] it was decided to establish a Coordinating Committee which would hold meetings under the auspices of, and in co-operation with, what at that time was the Centre for Human Rights and, in close co-operation with it, assist national institutions to follow up the relevant resolutions and recommendations concerning the strengthening of national institutions.[22] This was consolidated in the UN Commission on Human Rights' Resolution in March 1994.[23] This International Coordinating Committee (ICC) was duly established and functions in a number of ways. It co-ordinates NHRIs at the national level and encourages co-operation among them, through organising the ICC conferences and assisting with the regional ones.[24] It also ensures regular contacts with the OHCHR and other international organisations.[25] The work of the ICC is key to understanding the role of NHRIs in the UN structures. The ICC is composed of sixteen NHRIs, four from each of four regions 'for the purpose of ensuring a fair balance of regional representation on the ICC.'[26] These are the Americas, Africa, Asia-Pacific and Europe, institutions who themselves have to be accredited. They each elect one member to represent them on the ICC. The Chair and Vice Chair are chosen from among those sixteen members. As at the time of writing, the following African NHRIs are members of the ICC: Malawi, Morocco, Nigeria and Rwanda.

The ICC has been positioned increasingly within UN activities, rather than separate from them. This is even more apparent since the OHCHR provided secretarial support to the ICC through its National Institutions Unit, which replaced the Special Advisor previously created. Although recognising the support that this unit has provided to the ICC and NHRIs generally, due to the closeness of the relationship between the ICC and the OHCHR, there have been concerns voiced by NHRIs that the NI Unit is now acting beyond providing mere secretarial support for the ICC, to directing more what NHRIs should be doing. At the 17th session of the ICC various NHRIs raised the question about whether the secretariat of the ICC would be better placed permanently outside the UN structure and some expressed concerns that documents distributed by

[21] Second International Workshop on National Institutions for the Promotion and Protection of Human Rights, Tunis, 13–17 December 1993.

[22] E/CN.4/1994/45 and Add.1.

[23] UN Commission on Human Rights, Resolution 1994/94, 4 March 1994.

[24] International Coordinating Committee of National Institutions for the Promotion and Protection of Human Rights, Rules of Procedure, r 2.

[25] Ibid.

[26] Rules of Procedure of the ICC, above n 24, r 4(a).

the NI Unit reflected the view that it was the NI Unit that was directing NHRIs rather than the other way round.[27]

It is the ICC's Sub-Committee on Accreditation that makes recommendations to the ICC members as a whole on compliance of applications by NHRIs with the Paris Principles.[28] The decision on whether an NHRI is accredited or not increasingly has implications for the role that that NHRIs can then play at the international, and to a certain extent, the regional levels. The Sub-Committee on Accreditation is composed of one ICC accredited NHRI for each of the four regions, in order to ensure 'a fair balance of regional representation.'[29] They sit for two years and one of the members is chosen to act as chair. The Regional Grouping Representative has a role to assist NHRIs applying for accreditation from that region and give them the necessary information to do so.[30] The accreditation procedure will be dealt with fully in chapter 6. As at the time of writing there are 60 NHRIs in total with full accreditation by the ICC,[31] of which 17 are from Africa.

It is the accreditation by this ICC Sub-Committee that has influenced the extent to which NHRIs then participate in the UN Charter mechanisms. Nowhere is this more so than before the UN Human Rights Commission. Prior to the 61st session, representatives of NHRIs could participate as observers on the basis of letters from their institutions. This was possible irrespective of whether the NHRI had been accredited by Sub-Committee of ICC. Before and during the 61st session of the Human Rights Commission, NHRIs could only make oral statements in a very special item agenda item 18(b).

The procedure was then amended through the adoption of Commission Resolution 2005/74, requesting the Chair of the 61st session, in consultation with all stakeholders, to finalise by the 62nd session modalities for:

— 'permitting national institutions that are accredited by the Accreditation Subcommittee of the International Coordinating Committee of National Institutions under the auspices of the Office of the High Commissioner, and coordinating committees of such institutions, to speak, as outlined in the report, within their mandates, under all items of the Commission's agenda, while stressing the need to maintain present good practices of management of the agenda and speaking times in the Commission, to allocate dedicated

[27] Eg the Commission of Kenya noted the phrase in the ICC biannual work plan, distributed by the NI Unit, that the 'ICC shall work under the auspices of the OHCHR' should be amended to read: 'the ICC shall work with the UN HCHR,' ICC, Draft ICC Work Plan 2006, 17th Session of the International Co-ordinating Committee of NHRIs, 10–11 April 2006, on file with author.

[28] In 2005 the members of the Sub-Committee were Canada, Denmark, Fiji (acting Chair) and Uganda. The OHCHR can participate in the meetings as permanent observer, Rules of Procedure of the ICC Sub-Committee on Accreditation, as adopted by the members of the International Coordinating Committee at its 15th session, Seoul, Republic of Korea, 14 September 2004, para 2.4.

[29] Africa, Americas, Asia-Pacific and Europe, Rules of Procedure of the ICC Sub-Committee on Accreditation, ibid, at para 2.1.

[30] Ibid, at paras 3.1–3.2.

[31] Commission on Human Rights, above n 13, at para 9.

seating to national institutions for this purpose and supporting their engagement with all the subsidiary bodies of the Commission.'[32]

—maintaining good practices re speaking times in the Commission (at that time this was 7 minutes);
—allocation of specific seats;
—continuing the practice of issuing NHRI documentation under their own symbols.[33]

As regards those who were not accredited by the ICC, it was agreed that NHRIs should be allowed to speak under agenda item 18(b) and not across all agenda items. They were only allowed to make one statement lasting 7 minutes and copies of the report could be given out, as well as information on their regional meetings. A reason for only permitting NHRIs to speak on one agenda item was said to be due to the lack of time available overall.[34]

In the time that this procedure operated, NHRIs did use these opportunities and participated separately and as regional groupings,[35] although the discussion on item 18(b) was often not very helpful and could be made more directioned and efficient. In 2006 the Secretary-General of the UN adopted a report analysing the process of the ICC to accredit NHRIs in which it stressed the 'need for coordination of NHRI interventions on agenda items was emphasized, as was the importance of not necessarily intervening on all agenda items, but rather focusing on areas of particular interest.'[36]

Given the abolition of the UN Human Rights Commission shortly after in March 2006 and its replacement by a new Human Rights Council, so far there has been limited opportunity for NHRIs to use the procedures fully. What was clear, however, was that the trend up until this point has been that 'the accreditation of national institutions in international forums could be commensurate with the institution's accreditation to the ICC.'[37]

[32] Human Rights Commission, Resolution National Institutions for the Promotion and Protection of Human Rights, Resolution 2005/74, para 11(a).

[33] They have been allowed to circulate their own materials at other international events, such as at the Vienna Conference (papers circulated referenced with the prefix: A/CONF.157/NI/).

[34] Enhancing the Participation of National Human Rights Institutions in the Work of the Commission on Human Rights and its Subsidiary Bodies, above n 16, at para 22.

[35] Eg at the 61st session of the UN Human Rights Commission, the Coordinating Committee of African National Human Rights Institutions gave a statement, Statement from the Coordinating Committee of African National Human Rights Institutions. Presented at the 61st Session of the UN Commission on Human Rights by Margaret Sekaggya, Chairperson, Uganda Human Rights Commission / Chairperson Coordinating Committee of the African National Human Rights Institutions, Geneva, April 2005.

[36] Process currently utilised by the International Coordinating Committee to Accredit National Human Rights Institutions in compliance with the Paris Principles and ensure that the Process is Strengthened with Appropriate Periodic Review and on Ways and Means of Enhancing Participation of National Human Rights Institutions in the Work of the Commission, Report of the Secretary General, 25 January 2006, E/CN.4/2006/102, para 5.

[37] Ibid, at para 22.

Although the Secretary-General of the UN has said that this position should be the same with respect to NHRIs appearing before the subsidiary organs of the UN,[38] this has not yet been consistently applied. So, despite recognising the existence of these institutions,[39] the different subsidiary organs have taken different stances to their participation. For example, at the 55th session of the Sub-Commission on the Promotion and Protection of Human Rights NHRIs 'could be accredited to its sessions in their own right and speak on any substantive agenda item.'[40] In contrast, the Commission on the Status of Women does not provide standing for NHRIs in their own right and they have to attend as part of government delegations.[41]

Furthermore, the special procedures mandate holders of the Commission on Human Rights, 'increasingly consult with NHRI representatives and are an important mechanism in encouraging compliance with the Paris Principles and in providing support to NHRIs.'[42] Indeed, there have been suggestions made for how to increase this collaboration,[43] including that Special Procedures mandate holders could 'advocate for the establishment or strengthening of independent and credible NIs during their country visits, expressing support for NIs when relevant and calling to task NIs when they were not fulfilling their mandates. With their expertise, mandate holders could also provide advice to NIs in specific areas and take appropriate action when NIs were under threat.'[44] Some mandate holders look to NHRIs to assist in follow up of their recommendations.[45] Others have not displayed such a welcoming approach.

[38] Enhancing the Participation of National Human Rights Institutions in the Work of the Commission on Human Rights and its Subsidiary Bodies, above n 16.

[39] Eg the 9th session of the Working Group on Minorities in 2003 recommended governments set up such NHRIs with a remit over minority rights issues for state and non-state violations, E/CN.4/Sub.2/2003/19. This was reaffirmed at its 10th session, E/CN.4/Sub.2/2004/29.

[40] Effective Functioning of Human Rights Mechanisms: National Institutions and Regional Arrangements, above n 13, at para 14.

[41] Ibid, at para 16.

[42] Ibid, at para 67.

[43] It was noted that in June 2004 the NI Unit of the OHCHR would 'brief Special Procedures mandate holders during their annual meeting in order to support greater interaction between the Special Procedures mechanisms and Nis,' UN OHCHR, Member States Meeting Geneva, 28–29 June 2004. National Institutions Activities, January–June 2004, 16 June 2004, at 17.

[44] It was then noted that the mandate holders 'acknowledged the important role played by NIs in some countries but also called for vigilance in ensuring that the international community worked with credible institutions which operated in a truly independent capacity for the promotion and protection of human rights,' Report of the United Nations High Commissioner for Human Rights and Follow up to the World Conference on Human Rights. Effective Functioning of Human Rights Mechanisms, Note by the United Nations High Commissioner for Human Rights, E/CN.4/2005/5, 5 July 2004, paras 69 and 70.

[45] Effective Functioning of Human Rights Mechanisms: National Institutions and Regional Arrangements, above n 13, at para 68.

THE POSITION UNDER THE NEW HUMAN RIGHTS COUNCIL

In March 2006 the Commission on Human Rights sat for the last time and was replaced by a new Human Rights Council.[46] This Human Rights Council is a subsidiary organ of the General Assembly and composed of 47 member states with equitable geographical distribution.[47] Membership requires that states uphold 'the highest standards in the promotion and protection of human rights' and it can be suspended if the state commits 'gross and systematic violations of human rights.'[48] The Council has a wide remit to promote universal respect for all human rights, address situations of violations and make recommendations, and co-ordinate and mainstream human rights within the UN. Part of its mandate is to undertake a universal periodic review of each state's compliance with human rights obligations. The Council is to review the various mechanisms and functions of the Commission on Human Rights 'in order to maintain a system of special procedures, expert advice and a complaint procedure.'[49] It meets three times a year and met for the first time in June 2006. Leaving aside the criticisms already directed towards the new Council,[50] the Resolution establishing the Council lays out general provisions that are of relevance to the future participation of NHRIs in its work. The Resolution thus provides that the Council will 'assume the role and responsibilities of the Commission on Human Rights relating to the work of the Office of the United Nations High Commissioner for Human Rights,'[51] as well as 'work in close cooperation in the field of human rights with governments, regional organizations, national human rights institutions and civil society.'[52]

The Council has yet to adopt its own Rules of Procedure and it is likely that it will operate under the Rules established by the General Assembly for its Committees.[53] These Rules do not provide for participation of non-members, so this has to be based on General Assembly Resolution 251, the relevant paragraph of which reads: 'participation of and consultation with observers, including . . . national human rights institutions . . . shall be based on arrangements . . . and practices observed by the Commission on Human Rights, while ensuring the most effective contribution of these entities.'[54] It is not unreason-

[46] Resolution of the General Assembly, A/RES/60/251. ECOSOC Resolution 2006/2, Implementation of General Assembly Resolution 60/251, 'decides to abolish the Commission on Human Rights with effect on 16 June 2006,' para 2.

[47] Members were elected to the Council on 9 May 2006.

[48] A/RES/60/251, n.46, at paras 9 and 8 respectively.

[49] Ibid, at para 6.

[50] See, eg Human Rights Watch, 'UN: New Council Must Champion Fight for Rights,' 10 May 2006, http://hrw.org/english/docs/2006/05/10/global13343.htm.

[51] A/RES/60/251, above n 46, at para 5(g).

[52] Ibid, at para 5(h).

[53] Namely rr 98–133.

[54] A/RES/60/251, n.46, at para 11.

able to presume that the Rules applicable to the participation of NHRIs may also depend on the future structure, agenda and format of the sessions of the Council. There is a clear connection between how NHRIs have been dealt with by the UN Human Rights Commission and with how they will be considered by the new Council. Thus, the ICC have envisaged that regulation of NHRIs as defined by UN Commission on Human Rights resolutions will 'be transferred to the role of NHRIs in the Council on Human Rights.'[55] The Human Rights Commission has transmitted all its reports to the new Council which now has an obligation to consider them. Inevitably this includes the reports 2006/101 and 2006/102 relevant to the relationship with NHRIs. NHRIs find it encouraging that some states have already committed their support to NHRIs in their pledges in support of their candidacies.[56]

Despite this, although NHRIs are unlikely to be invisible in the new Council, as Chris Sidoti noted at the 17th session of the International Coordinating Committee, the present position poses both 'risks and opportunities.' So far, however, NHRIs themselves have not considered going further than the approach outlined in Resolution 2005/74, namely that the ICC takes the following position with respect to NHRIs in the Human Rights Council:

—NHRIs should participate in the Human Rights Council sessions in the same way as reflected in Commission on Human Rights Resolution 2005/74.
—The Human Rights Council should establish a mechanism which allows NHRIs to raise issues of special concern with the Council.
—The Human Rights Council is strongly encouraged to establish a focal point for the protection of human rights defenders, which should interact closely with the ICC in relation to the protection of NHRIs and their members, including in relation to threats against them.[57]

The ICC is also advocating that NHRIs participate in the universal periodic review, including giving information on how states have fulfilled their international obligations, being able to speak in the interactive dialogue with the state, and be included on the agenda where country missions are envisaged.[58] With respect to the Special Procedures, the ICC proposed that NHRIs should submit information and documentation to them where issues of specific concern

[55] 17th Session of the International Coordinating Committee of NHRIs, Agenda item 9a–9d. The Role of NHRIs in the UN System. Discussion Paper on NHRIs in the UN Reform Process, para 1.1.

[56] Eg Algeria, http://www.un.org/ga/60/elect/hrc/algeria.pdf; Gabon, http://www.un.org/ga/60/elect/hrc/gabon.pdf; Ghana, http://www.un.org/ga/60/elect/hrc/ghana.pdf; Mauritius, http://www.un.org/ga/60/elect/hrc/mauritius.pdf; Morocco, http://www.un.org/ga/60/elect/hrc/morocco.pdf; Nigeria, http://www.un.org/ga/60/elect/hrc/nigeria.pdf; Senegal, http://www.un.org/ga/60/elect/hrc/senegal.pdf; South Africa, http://www.un.org/ga/60/elect/hrc/southafrica.pdf; Tunisia, http://www.un.org/ga/60/elect/hrc/tunisia.pdf; and Zambia, http://www.un.org/ga/60/elect/hrc/zambia.pdf.

[57] 17th Session of the International Coordinating Committee of NHRIs, Agenda item 9a–9d. The Role of NHRIs in the UN System, above n 55, at para 1.2.1.

[58] Ibid, at para 1.2.2.

arise, and that NHRIs should be included in the agenda of country missions and be given information about them on time.[59]

The role of NHRIs before the Human Rights Council is clearly crucial. It is possible that the position as suggested by Resolution 60/251 could simply be adopted by the new Human Rights Council. However, there is a risk that NHRIs will have a lesser status, particularly if there are concerns over the accreditation procedure by the ICC. Compared with NGOs, whose status through ECOSOC Resolution 1996/31[60] has been implemented over many years and is consolidated in practice, albeit not without its limitations, NHRIs may be in a more vulnerable position, being relatively recent additions to the international playing field. Without considerable lobbying by NHRIs themselves it is possible that their position could be weaker than at present. On the other hand, however, with some effort, NHRI could use this opportunity to enhance their position above and beyond that provided in Resolution 2005/74. If NHRIs can justify their involvement in international and regional forums and provide ways of making themselves accountable, they may in fact end up with more than proposed under the Human Rights Commission.

BEFORE UN TREATY MECHANISMS AND AT UN CONFERENCES

There are currently seven treaty bodies established under the UN system,[61] although additional bodies on disability and disappearances have been proposed.[62] The NI Unit at the OHCHR has assisted NHRIs in engaging with treaty bodies[63] and has a member of staff specifically assigned to the relation-

[59] 7th Session of the International Coordinating Committee of NHRIs, Agenda item 9a–9d. The Role of NHRIs in the UN System, above n 55, at para 1.2.3.

[60] 25 July 1996.

[61] These are the Human Rights Committee (ICCPR), Committee on Economic, Social and Cultural Rights (ICESCR), Committee on the Elimination of All Forms of Discrimination Against Women (CEDAW), Committee on the Elimination of Racial Discrimination (ICERD), Committee Against Torture (UNCAT), Committee on the Rights of the Child (UNCRC), and the Committee on Migrant Workers (International Convention on the Protection of the Rights of all Migrant Workers and Members of their Families).

[62] Art 33(2) of the working text of the Convention provides that 'States parties shall, in accordance with their legal and administrative systems, maintain, strengthen, designate or establish at the national level an independent mechanism to promote, protect and monitor implementation of the present Convention, taking into account, where necessary, gender and age specific issues. When designating or establishing such a mechanism, States Parties shall take into account the Principles relating to the status and functioning of national institutions for protection and promotion of human rights.'

[63] Eg through training programmes, UN OHCHR, First Quarterly Public Report for 2005, National Institutions Activities, January–March 2005, March 2005. There have also been a series of workshops held under an ongoing European Union-funded project on 'Strengthening the implementation of human rights treaty recommendations through the enhancement of national protection mechanisms,' Effective Functioning of Human Rights Mechanisms: National Institutions and Regional Arrangements, above n 13, at para 61.

ship between treaty bodies and NHRIs.[64] Compilations of the concluding observations and decisions of treaty bodies have been posted on the NHRI website and the NI Unit also sends these to NHRIs in the countries concerned.[65] Unlike before the UN Human Rights Commission and its subsidiary bodies, recognition of the role of NHRIs in treaty body mechanisms looked less at their accreditation by the ICC. While several treaty bodies have recognised explicitly the role that NHRIs can play and encouraged forms of participation, the manner in which the treaty bodies have approached these institutions has not been consistent. As the UN NI Unit admits:

> there are no set, clear procedures concerning national institutions' engagement with treaty bodies. Rather each treaty body has to date made its own determination regarding such engagement.[66]

Some treaty bodies have been proactive in the amount of involvement they have permitted NHRIs or attention they have given to them in their work, despite only one of them expressly referring to NHRIs in its Rules of Procedure.[67] The Committee on the Rights of the Child, for example, in what has been described as a model approach,[68] has adopted a detailed General Comment on the Role of Independent National Human Rights Institutions in the Promotion and Protection of the Rights of the Child,[69] in which it noted the importance of NHRIs to 'promote and ensure the implementation of the Convention, and the Committee on the Rights of the Child (CRC) considers the establishment of such bodies to fall within the commitment made by states parties upon ratification to ensure the implementation of the Convention and advance the universal realization of children's rights'[70] It thus encouraged states to set up an independent

[64] UN OHCHR, First Quarterly Public Report for 2005, ibid, at 7–8; Effective Functioning of Human Rights Mechanisms: National Institutions and Regional Arrangements, above n 13, at para 60.

[65] Effective Functioning of Human Rights Mechanisms: National Institutions and Regional Arrangements, above n 13, at para 66.

[66] NI Unit, *The United Nations Treaty Bodies and National Institutions*, http://www.nhri.net/pdf/TBs_and_NIs.pdf, 2.

[67] R 29 of the Provisional Rules of Procedure of the Committee on the Protection of the Rights of All Migrant Workers and Members of Their Families states: 'In accordance with article 74, paragraph 4, of the Convention, the Committee may invite specialized agencies and organs of the United Nations, as well as intergovernmental organizations and other concerned bodies (including national human rights institutions, non-governmental organizations, and other bodies), to submit, for consideration by the Committee, written information on such matters dealt with in the Convention as fall within the scope of their activities,' HRI/GEN/3/Rev.2

[68] See comments of Brice Dickson, then chair of the Northern Ireland Human Rights Commission, Brice Dickson, Chief Commissioner, Northern Ireland Human Rights Commission, Address to the Workshop on the Paris Principles, Tirana, Albania, 5 May 2004, www.nihrc.org.

[69] General Comment No 2, The Role of Independent National Human Rights Institutions in the Promotion and Protection of the Rights of the Child, 31st session, 2002, HRI/GEN/1/Rev.7. Similarly, the Committee on the Elimination of Racial Discrimination has adopted a General Recommendation on the establishment of national institutions to facilitate implementation of the Convention, General Recommendation XVII on the establishment of national institutions to facilitate implementation of the Convention, 42nd session, 1993, HRI/GEN/1/Rev.7.

[70] General Comment No 2, ibid, at para 1.

institution to promote and monitor implementation of the CRC and for those already established, to review their status and effectiveness with respect to children's rights.[71] The Committee stresses compliance with the Paris Principles when establishing such bodies but goes further in the detail it lays out.[72] It makes some specific comments with respect to whether it would be more appropriate to have a separate commission or institutions for children rather than as being part of a general human rights institution,[73] and sets out the mandate and powers such a body should possess.[74]

Many UN treaty bodies have questioned states during the examination of their state reports on the independence of the institutions,[75] calling on them to increase the powers and resources provided to these institutions,[76] requiring them to provide more information[77] and encouraging states to establish such

[71] General Comment No 2, ibid, at para 2.

[72] Ibid, at para 4.

[73] Ibid, at paras 6 and 7.

[74] Including that it be 'constitutionally entrenched and must at least be legislatively mandated. . . . their mandate should include as board a scope as possible for promoting and protecting human rights . . . . NHRIs should be accorded such powers as are necessary to enable them to discharge their mandate effectively, including the power to hear any person and obtain any information and document necessary for assessing the situations falling within their competence,' ibid, at paras 8 and 9.

[75] Eg The Committee on the Elimination of Racial Discrimination in its Concluding Observations on the state report of Côte d'Ivoire at its 62nd session, 'recommends that the state party continue its efforts to adopt legislation or regulations which define the respective spheres of competence of the National Human Rights Commission and Ombudsman Office, spell out the procedure for bringing case before them and determine whether their decisions are binding. More specifically, the Committee invites the state party to strengthen the guarantees of independence of these bodies so that their activities will be effective and credible, particularly for the purposes of mediation. To this end, the state party should take the appropriate measures to inform the public of the remedies available to the victims of acts of discrimination of xenophobia,' 62nd session, CERD/C/62/CO/1, 3 June 2003, para 18. See also: examination of Cameroon's report before the Human Rights Committee, see Amnesty International, 'Cameroon fails to protect the fundamental human rights of its citizens', AI Index: AFR 17/06/99, 9 November 1999; Concluding Observations of the Committee on the Elimination of Racial Discrimination in respect of Chad's 2003 report, A/48/18, 42nd session of the CERD Committee, para 165.

[76] Eg Concluding Observations on Zimbabwe's report, at its 56th session, the Committee on the Elimination of Racial Discrimination expressed its concern with the restricted powers of the Ombudsman to investigate acts of public officials on issues of racial discrimination and to limit access to complaints processes, recommended that the state take action to allow her to do so, CERD/C/304/Add.92, 19 April 2000, para 8.

[77] Eg in its Concluding Observations on Rwanda at its 56th session, the Committee on the Elimination of Racial Discrimination asked the state in its next report to give more information on 'actions taken, and results achieved, by the National Human Rights Commission,' CERD/C/304/Add.97, 19 April 2000, para 20(c). Similarly, in its Concluding Observations on Mauritius at its 57th session, the Committee on the Elimination of Racial Discrimination noted that 'since the National Human Rights Commission and the Committee on Poverty are very recent institutions, the state party is also invited, in its next report, to provide further information on their functioning and the results of their activities, with particular reference to problems of racial discrimination,' 57th session, CERD/C/304/Add.106, 1 May 2001, para 10. See also: Concluding Observations on Algeria at its 58th session, the Committee on the Elimination of Racial Discrimination, 58th session, CERD/C/304/Add.113, 27 April 2001, para 16.

where none exist.[78] They have also advocated for an enhanced role for some institutions,[79] in some cases encouraging the establishment of NHRIs with specific powers relevant to the particular treaty. For example, the Committee on the Rights of the Child when examining Côte d'Ivoire's initial report under the UN Convention on the Rights of the Child, encouraged it to set up an independent NHRI 'to monitor and evaluate progress in the implementation of the Convention at the national level and, if appropriate, at the local level. In addition, the institution should be empowered to receive and investigate complaints of violations of child rights in a child-sensitive manner, and effectively address them. The Committee encourages the state party to seek technical assistance from, among others, OHCHR and UNICEF.'[80]

[78] Eg in its Concluding Observations on Egypt at its 59th session, the Committee on the Elimination of Racial Discrimination noted that the state was in the process of setting up 'a National Council for Human Rights in accordance with the Paris Principles . . . the Committee recommends that steps be taken to accelerate this process and requests the State party to provide information on the powers and functions of this institution in its next periodic report,' 59th session, A/56/18, para 292. Similarly, in its Concluding Observations on Sudan at its 23rd session, the Committee on Economic, Social and Cultural Rights noted 'in the light of the recent establishment of committees addressing specific human rights issues, the Committee encourages the state party to establish an independent national human rights institution, in accordance with the 1991 Paris Principles,' 23rd session, E/C.12/1/Add.48, 1 September 2000, para 31. See also Concluding Observations on Togo at its 25th session, Committee on Economic, Social and Cultural Rights 25th session, E/C.12/1/Add.61, 21 May 2001, para 9; Gabon's second periodic report before the Human Rights Committee, Human Rights Committee, List of Issues: Gabon, 17/08/2000, CCPR/C/70/L/GAB, 17 August 2000, para 2; CEDAW General Recommendation No 6, 7th session, 1988, Effective National Machinery and Publicity, at para 1. In its Concluding Observations on Egypt at its 22nd session, the Committee on Economic, Social and Cultural Rights urged that state to establish an NHRI which was in conformity with the Paris Principles, 22nd session, E/C.12/1/Add.44, 23 May 2000, para 30.

[79] The Committee on the Rights of the Child noted that states should consider establishing a review procedure for dealing with complaints of violations of Art 29(1) of the CRC, which might be 'entrusted to national human rights institutions or to existing administrative bodies,' General Comment Adopted by the Committee on the Rights of the Child, 26th session, 2001, General Comment No 1: The Aims of Education, para 25.

[80] Committee on the Rights of the Child, Concluding Observations of the Committee on the Rights of the Child: Côte d'Ivoire, 9 July 2001, CRC/C/15/Add.155, paras 12 - 13. A similar recommendation is made to Tunisia, although it also adds that such an NHRI should also include implementation 'by the private sector and NGOs as providers of services to children,' Committee on the Rights of the Child, Concluding Observations of the Committee on the Rights of the Child: Tunisia, 16 June 2002, CRC/C/15/Add.181, paras 16–17. This appears to have been a previous issue raised with respect to earlier reports submitted to the Committee. Similar recommendations were made to Egypt, noting the existence of the NCCM, Committee on the Rights of the Child, Concluding Observations of the Committee on the Rights of the Child: Egypt, 21 February 2001, CRC/C/15/Add.145, para 17. The Committee on the Rights of the Child list of issues with respect to Equatorial Guinea's initial periodic report included a request for information on 'the creation of an independent monitoring body, such as a National Human Rights Institution,' Committee on the Rights of the Child, List of Issues: Equatorial Guinea, 11 June 2004, CRC/C/Q/GNQ/1, para B.4. The Committee on the Rights of the Child also listed this among the issues for Sao Tome and Principe in their initial report, Committee on the Rights of the Child, List of Issues: Sao Tome and Principe, 13 February 2004, CRC/C/Q/STP/1, para B.4. Similarly, the Committee on the Rights of the Child in its Concluding Observations on the Initial Report of Cape Verde to the UN CRC noted 'while noting the recent establishment of the National Commission on Human Rights and its subcommissions, the Committee is concerned at the absence of an effective and independent mechanism for monitoring the Convention's implementation. The Committee recommends that the state party consider the establishment of an independent national human rights institution in accordance with

NHRIs have also been supported in their work by treaty bodies[81] which have called on governments to comply with the NHRIs' recommendations and allow the NHRIs to function effectively. For example, in its Concluding Observations on Kenya at its 28th session, the Committee on the Elimination of Discrimination Against Women (CEDAW) noted its concern that the National Commission on Gender and Development,

> is lacking the means to effectively coordinate among the different mechanisms related to gender; and that the lack of a clear division of responsibilities and insufficient budget allocations may have a negative bearing on the effective implementation of the Convention. The Committee recommends that the state party clearly define the mandate and responsibilities of the different mechanisms related to the advancement of women and gender equality and allocate sufficient budgetary resources to them.[82]

Indeed, many treaty bodies have expressed the importance that NHRIs, acting 'as a bridge between civil society and government national institutions can encourage state ratification and also sensitise the public of the need for such ratification to bring further pressure on the state.'[83]

NHRIs have been encouraged to play some role in the state reporting process. However, as chapter 6 indicates, this poses a number of tensions that have yet to be fully resolved. Beyond this, NHRIs have been asked to follow up the recommendations and decisions of the treaty bodies,[84] contribute in the drafting of the list of issues, participate in training,[85] pre-sessional working groups and in briefings before meetings,[86] and follow up on concluding observations once

the Principles relating to the status of national institutions for the promotion and protection of human rights. . . . to monitor and evaluate progress in the implementation of the Convention at the national and local levels. This institution should be accessible to children and empowered to receive and investigate complaints of violations of child rights in a child-sensitive manner and to address them effectively. Consider the development of a focal point on children's rights within the National Commission on Human Rights,' Committee on the Rights of the Child, Concluding Observations of the Committee on the Rights of the Child: Cape Verde, 7 November 2001, CRC/C/15/Add.168, paras 16–17.

[81] Eg in its Concluding Observations on Cameroon's state report, the Committee Against Torture noted 'with satisfaction . . . the promise by the representatives of the state party to permit the national Commission on Human Rights to visit detention centres on the terms recommended by the Special Rapporteur,' 25th session, A/56/44, para 63(f). In its Concluding Observations on the Mali at its 77th session, the Human Rights Committee 'notes with concern that the National Advisory Commission on Human Rights, established in 1996, is yet to meet. The state party should take appropriate measures to allow the National Advisory Commission on Human Rights to function, in accordance with the . . . Paris Principles,' 77th session, CCPR/CO/77/MLI, 16 April 2003, para 8.

[82] 28th session, 13–31 January 2003, Supplement No 38, A/58/38, paras 225–26.

[83] NI Unit, above n 66, at 2.

[84] Ibid. The CERD Committee has also called on national human rights institutions to 'assist their respective states to comply with their reporting obligations and closely monitor the follow-up to the concluding observations and recommendations of the Committee,' General Recommendation XXVIII on the follow-up to the World Conference Against Racism, Racial Discrimination, Xenophobia and Related Intolerance, 60th session of CERD Committee, 2002, HRI/GEN/1/Rev.7, para 2(a).

[85] NI Unit, above n 66, at 5.

[86] Although the practicalities of doing so are not yet set out, NI Unit, above n 66, at 2.

adopted by the treaty bodies.[87] However, the extent to which these various tasks are carried out and encouraged by each treaty body is not systematic.[88]

The existing treaty system raises a number of issues for NHRIs. Given the different approaches by each treaty body on how to communicate and participate with them, inconsistency in access to the various treaty bodies, and no systematic system of follow up by treaty bodies,[89] it is difficult for NHRIs to develop any coherent policy on their relationship with the bodies as a whole. There is some hope, however, that with changes being proposed to the treaty body mechanisms a more consistent approach to NHRIs can be developed. For example, where treaty bodies have met in an inter-committee forum, they have recognised the need to engage more with NHRIs. At the inter-committee meeting of treaty bodies in June 2005 several representatives of NHRIs, including from Uganda, participated.[90] During discussions the inter-committee stressed the need for greater co-operation between NHRIs and treaty bodies and noted that this cooperation had already begun: 'some had requested information from those institutions during the preparation of lists of issues, during the pre-sessional working groups, or in the plenary sessions. It was hoped that such practices would be adopted by all treaty bodies in a unified manner.'[91] It was noted here that given the different mandates and backgrounds of NHRIs, members of the inter-committee felt that some issues should be considered in their interaction with these institutions, including, in particular, compliance with the Paris Principles, the need for NHRIs to be independent and not be part of government delegations to treaty body sessions, with most of the treaty bodies calling for NHRIs to be able to make independent statements.[92] Although it has been recommended that NHRIs attend future inter-committee meetings and that the inter-committee consider joint criteria for the participation of NHRIs in the work of treaty bodies,[93] beyond this it would seem that there is the possibility for NHRIs to carve out some role for themselves at this level. The inter-committee did make it clear, however, that if the ICC Sub-Committee on Accreditation were to be strengthened it could address concerns of treaty bodies about how NHRIs should participate.[94]

The proposals for a Unified Standing Treaty Body have a number of implications for NHRIs and their manner of participation with treaty mechanisms. A

[87] Ibid, at 2–3.

[88] Ibid, at 5.

[89] 17th session of the International Coordinating Committee of NHRIs, Agenda item 9a–9d. The Role of NHRIs in the UN System, above n 55, at para 2.2.1.

[90] Effective Functioning of Human Rights Mechanisms: National Institutions and Regional Arrangements, above n 13, at para 64. See also Effective Functioning of International Instruments on Human Rights, including Reporting Obligations under International Instruments on Human Rights. Note by the Secretary-General, 19 August 2005, A/60/278, para 28.

[91] Effective Functioning of International Instruments on Human Rights, including Reporting Obligations under International Instruments on Human Rights, ibid, at para 30.

[92] Ibid, at para 31.

[93] Ibid, at paras XII, XIII, XIV.

[94] Ibid, at para 31.

Unified Standing Treaty body would be a permanent body.[95] Reporting by states would be done in the form of an initial expanded core document and a treaty specific report. Periodic reports would be abolished and instead states would have to respond to a list of specific issues on all treaty obligations. As states will only be examined by the body under the state reporting procedure every 4 or 5 years,[96] this may reduce the possibilities of NHRIs engaging regularly with it. With respect to communications, there would be one chamber to look at manifestly ill-founded cases and possible routine ones, and then a chamber for consideration of complaints which would be able to deal with violations of more than one treaty in one case. This unified body would also be able to appoint Special Rapporteurs for each treaty or for particular themes. The ICC has already expressed concern that 'insufficient expertise in each convention could lead to less specific and sharp recommendations making them more difficult to apply and implement at national level.'[97]

Despite the significant changes that the proposed Unified Standing Treaty Body suggests and besides some additional suggestions that NHRIs should be more involved in discussions on thematic issues and consultations on general comments,[98] and submit cases themselves to the treaty bodies,[99] the ICC has been fairly conservative in its approach, advocating little more involvement than is already the case, albeit on a more systematic basis. It has thus argued that NHRIs should be able to submit shadow reports or other documentation relating to state reports,[100] give interventions on state reports,[101] enable civil society to be part of consultations,[102] be involved in site visits,[103] give information on recommendations and engage with civil society and government on follow up,[104] and be able to submit information re early warning.[105] Although those working on the treaty body mechanisms have recognised that there is 'absolutely no reason why there should be this difference in approach' between the treaty bodies in terms of their treatment of NHRIs,[106] there has not been any real consideration, by the ICC or treaty bodies, of the position of NHRIs as state or non-state actors.

[95] Concept Paper on the High Commissioner's Proposal for a Unified Standing Treaty Body, Report by the Secretariat, HRI/MC/2006/CRP.1, 14 March 2006.

[96] 17th session of the International Coordinating Committee of NHRIs, Agenda item 9a–9d. The Role of NHRIs in the UN System, above n 55, at para 2.2.1.

[97] Ibid.

[98] Ibid, at para 2.2.2.

[99] Where domestic remedies have been exhausted, ibid, at para 2.2.2.

[100] Ibid.

[101] Ibid.

[102] Ibid.

[103] Ibid.

[104] Ibid.

[105] Ibid.

[106] Jane Connors at the 17th session of the ICC in April 2006.

At the 17th session of the ICC it was decided to establish two working groups to consider the role of NHRIs in the treaty bodies,[107] and the role of NHRIs in the new Human Rights Council.[108] These reported back to the 18th session of the ICC in October 2006. They did little more than look at the current position and encourage the Human Rights Council and treaty bodies to 'seek the participation and input of NHRIs' into their work[109] and did not take a wider perspective to examine the role of NHRIs in general and how they can fit, coherently, within the international forums.

OTHER INTERNATIONAL FORA

Although the focus of the NHRIs attention and that of the ICC has been on ensuring the involvement and recognition by the UN Charter and treaty body mechanisms, there has been some, albeit limited, discussion about the possible role NHRIs could have in other UN organs and international institutions,[110] such as the General Assembly of the UN, ECOSOC, as well as specialised agencies.[111] The difficulties here lie in the fact that each organ has different rules regarding participation and that the amount of participation of NHRIs may depend on how many resources NHRIs have to interact at this level. For example, there is no reference in the Rules of Procedure of the General Assembly[112] to NHRIs and, as was noted by John von Doussa of the Australian NHRI at the 17th session of the ICC, to push for participation in this arena would be seen as particularly radical: 'To be pragmatic, some states, those without National Institutions, would not want to give those with National Institutions a second bite of the cherry, and those with National Institutions were likely to show some resistance to the prospect of their National Institution criticising their own states in that forum. There may also be opposition as it would impose another layer of interventions on the system.' He cautioned against NHRIs participating at the General Assembly at this stage on the grounds that it 'might backfire and

[107] This is composed of NHRIs from Germany, Kenya and one from the Americas, and Asia-Pacific.

[108] This is composed of NHRIs from France, Morocco, Mexico and Venezuela, and Asia-Pacific.

[109] International Coordinating Committee of National Human Rights Institutions (ICC), *ICC Position Papers. National Human Rights Institutions and the UN Human Rights Council, Volume I*, 27 June 2006, www.nhri.net, at para 4; International Coordinating Committee of National Human Rights Institutions (ICC), *ICC Position Papers. National Human Rights Institutions and the UN Human Rights Council, Volume II: National Human Rights Institutions and the Special Procedures and Universal Periodic Review Mechanism*, 22 September 2006, www.nhri.net.

[110] 17th session of the International Coordinating Committee of NHRIs, Agenda item 9a–9d. The Role of NHRIs in the UN System, above n 55, at para 3.

[111] John von Doussa, President of the Australian Human Rights and Equality Commission noted at the 17th session of the ICC that some APF members met on this issue with ambassadors of their own states, and the latter said they were looking for assistance from National Institutions to understand the role that they could play.

[112] Rules of Procedure of the General Assembly, A/520/Rev.15, 1985.

provide ammunition to states wanting to limit our role.' There would be a need to negotiate with each sub-committee or working committee of the General Assembly, and with other organs. With respect to agencies under the United Nations Economics and Social Council (ECOSOC), the Commission on the Status of Women has not proved to be particularly open to participation of NHRIs.

Given that the ability of NHRIs to participate in the new Human Rights Council is likely to influence their ability to participate elsewhere, the ICC has advocated focusing on formulating interaction with the new Human Rights Council first, before considering how best to interact with these other bodies. This is a sensible approach. A similar caution should also be exercised when considering the potential for NHRI interaction in other organs and institutions such as the International Court of Justice, and institutions beyond the UN structure. Here, again, participation is likely to depend on a credible accreditation procedure which operates outside the domestic system.

CONCLUSION

The participation of NHRIs in the UN structures has a recent history and is not sufficiently established to guarantee its adoption by any new UN body. It is still very much open to debate what role NHRIs will play in the new structures of the UN. Yet, how this ends up being defined, particularly in respect of their participation in the new Human Rights Council, will be crucial for their participation in other meetings, whether at the UN or regionally. NHRIs see this as an opportunity now to enhance their role and status at this level, thus bringing benefits not only internationally but domestically.

Despite some recognition and efforts taken to strengthen the role of NHRIs since 2001, the Secretary-General of the UN has affirmed that 'the status of NIs and, accordingly, the nature of their participation in the work of the Commission and its subsidiary bodies have yet to be formally defined.'[113]

[113] Enhancing the Participation of National Human Rights Institutions in the Work of the Commission on Human Rights and its Subsidiary Bodies, above n 16.

4

NHRIs at the Regional Level

BESIDES INVOLVEMENT AND recognition at the UN, (National Human Rights Institutions (NHRIs) have also developed a role for themselves at the regional level.

THE AFRICAN UNION (AU)

Regionally, the African Union (AU) is the main political structure for the continent. This body, which replaced the Organization of African Unity (OAU) in 2001, provides in its Constitutive Act for a number of principal organs.[1] These include an Assembly of Heads of State, an Executive Council, composed of ministers of governments, as well as a Permanent Representatives' Committee. A Pan-African Parliament operates under the auspices of the AU, at present from South Africa, there is also a Peace and Security Council and an Economic, Social and Cultural Council (ECOSOCC), the latter intending to provide a formal structure by which civil society organisations and others can engage with the Union. The AU is served by a secretariat in Addis Ababa, namely its AU Commission, which includes eight individual Commissioners with remits over specific portfolios. From the perspective of human rights the most important of these is the Commissioner for Political Affairs.[2] There is also provision in the Constitutive Act for the establishment of an African Court of Justice, to act as the principal judicial organ of the AU, but it has yet to be established and its development is closely tied with that of the African Court on Human and Peoples' Rights.[3] Among the Objectives and Principles of the AU as stated in the Constitutive Act are significant references to human rights standards.[4] As a result the AU now has a specific mandate to focus on human rights issues.

Although the OAU paid limited attention to human rights, leaving this mainly to the African Commission on Human and Peoples' Rights, as will be discussed below, towards the end of the 1990s it displayed an increasing interest

[1] Constitutive Act of the African Union, 11 July 2000, Art 5.
[2] At present this is Julia Joyner from The Gambia.
[3] As outlined below.
[4] Arts 3 and 4 of the Constitutive Act.

in these issues.[5] This was marked in a number of ways, not least by the holding of ministerial level conferences on human rights in 1999 and again, under the AU, in 2003. Against this backdrop, although NHRIs had not been considered in any great detail by the AU organs, the outcomes of these ministerial human rights conferences did mention the role of NHRIs expressly. While stating that the 'primary responsibility for the promotion and protection of Human Rights lies with the State,' they urged states 'to establish national human rights institutions and to provide them with adequate financial resources and ensure their independence'[6] and stressed the need for co-operation between these NHRIs and the African Commission on Human and Peoples' Rights in order to 'greatly enhance respect for Human Rights in Africa.'[7]

Besides participating in the sessions of the African Commission on Human and Peoples' Rights, as outlined below, there has been little opportunity for NHRIs to engage at the level of the AU and its former organisation, the OAU. It is possible that more formal procedures under ECOSOCC could enable this to happen in the future. ECOSOCC is to promote dialogue between all sectors of African people, and 'forge strong partnerships between governments and all segments of the civil society.'[8] Its composition, defined as 'different social and professional groups of the Member States of the African Union' is potentially broad enough to include NHRIs, if they are seen as 'civil society' for this purpose.[9] As an advisory organ of the AU, if NHRIs participated in this Council they would have a regular mechanism through which to input their views.

A less formalised, but still significant, approach has been taken by the AU so far, with the holding of a conference specifically dedicated to NHRIs in October 2004[10] as 'the first in a series of activities envisaged by the AU in its vision, mission and strategic plan in order to contribute to the widespread establishment and capacity building of independent national human rights institutions in Africa.'[11] The aim of the conference, it was said, was to 'sustain the work being

[5] For a discussion of the role of human rights in the OAU and AU see R Murray, *Human Rights in Africa. From Organization of African Unity to African Union* (Cambridge, Cambridge University Press, 2004).

[6] Grand Bay (Mauritius) Declaration and Plan of Action, 12–16 April 1999, para 15. Similarly in the Kigali Declaration from the first AU Ministerial Conference on Human Rights in 2003 it again 'Reiterates that the primary responsibility for the promotion and protection of human rights rests with Member States and, therefore, urges those Member States which have not yet done so, to establish independent national human rights institutions, provide them with adequate financial and other resources for their proper functioning, and guarantee their independence,' Kigali Declaration, 8 May 2003, para 27.

[7] Grand Bay Declaration and Plan of Action, ibid, at para 23.

[8] Statutes of the Economic, Social and Cultural Council, PRC/ECOSOCC Statutes/Rev.5, Arts 2(1) and (2).

[9] Ibid, Art 3 under the definition of 'civil society organisation.'

[10] First African Union Conference of National Human Rights Institutions, 18–21 October 2004, Addis Ababa, Draft Report. On file with author. Final Communiqué. First African Union Conference of National Human Rights Institutions, 18–21 October 2004, Addis Ababa, Ethiopia.

[11] Draft Report on the First African Union Conference of National Human Rights Institutions, ibid, at 1.

done by existing national institutions and to promote the creation of new national institutions where they do not exist.'[12] It focused specifically on reviewing the Paris Principles, outlining the difficulties faced by NHRIs, identifying partnerships in Africa that NHRIs need to develop their agendas, and developing a strategy for implementing the Kigali Declaration. As elsewhere, the AU is thus still advocating that states establish NHRIs where none exist.[13] The Final Communiqué of the conference reaffirmed 'the need for better cooperation among NHRIs, the African Union and its organs, the African Commission on Human and Peoples' Rights, non-governmental organisations, and other institutions with human rights agendas.'[14] Besides calling on NHRIs to ensure that governments comply with their international human rights obligations, it also called on them to apply for affiliated status with the African Commission and to attend its sessions.[15] The Commission of the AU was also given the specific task to 'speak out on behalf of National Human Rights Institutions to their respective governments, to provide them with juristic, material and financial resources to enable them to effectively carry out their mandates.'[16] Non-African States, the international community and international NGOs were also called upon to 'recognise the legitimacy of NHRIs.'[17] It was intended to hold the conference on a biannual basis.

While many welcomed this recognition of the role that NHRIs could play in the AU, concerns were expressed at the lack of involvement in the conference of the African Commission on Human and Peoples' Rights. At present, it is unlikely, however, that the AU will do little beyond holding the conferences on NHRIs. Where there is more regular contact, it is in relation to the AU's main human rights body, the African Commission on Human and Peoples' Rights.

THE AFRICAN COMMISSION ON HUMAN AND PEOPLES' RIGHTS

The majority of the focus of human rights work of the previous OAU and present AU, has fallen to the main human rights treaty for the continent, the African Charter on Human and Peoples' Rights. Adopted in 1981 and coming into force in 1986, it provides for an eleven member independent African Commission on Human and Peoples' Rights whose headquarters is in The Gambia. The Commission operates under a promotional and protective mandate,[18] including

[12] Ibid.

[13] Final Communiqué First African Union Conference of National Human Rights Institutions, above n 10, at para 17.

[14] Final Communiqué First African Union Conference of National Human Rights Institutions, ibid; Draft Report on the First African Union Conference of National Human Rights Institutions, above n 10, at 5, para 8.

[15] Final Communiqué First African Union Conference of National Human Rights Institutions, ibid, at 6, para 16.

[16] Ibid, at para 19,

[17] Ibid at 7, para 21.

[18] Art 45 ACHPR.

receiving reports from states on the measures they have taken to comply with the ACHPR[19]; making decisions on communications alleging violations of rights in the ACHPR, submitted by individuals, NGOs and others[20]; adopting resolutions on specific issues or countries; holding seminars in collaboration with others, and undertaking missions to state parties on a promotional or protective basis, among others. NGOs can apply for observer status with the African Commission and more recently the African Commission has adopted a similar process for the involvement of NHRIs.

Working on the principle in Article 45(1) of the African Charter,[21] and Article 26 of the African Charter that states 'shall allow the establishment and improvement of appropriate national institutions entrusted with the promotion and protection of the rights and freedoms guaranteed by the present Charter,' the African Commission has since 1998 found a formal position for NHRIs within its work. Although it recognised as early as 1989 the existence of such institutions to 'help governments solve their national or local problems relevant to human rights, thus promoting a better awareness of issues related to human rights,'[22] there was no real discussion of the role that they could play with the African Commission until 1997.[23] Given that some members of the African Commission were themselves members of NHRIs in their home countries, and spurred on with the adoption of the Paris Principles and the creation of the ICC, the relationship between NHRIs and the African Commission became of increasing interest to the extent that it then became a regular item on the agenda of each session.[24] At the 21st session in April 1997 one Commissioner presented a document on 'strengthening cooperation between the Commission and National Human Rights Institutions.'[25] Further discussion was postponed

[19] Art 62 ACHPR.

[20] Arts 47–54 provide for communications submitted by states, Arts 55–59 provide for communications submitted by others.

[21] This states that 'the functions of the Commission shall be: 1. To promote human and peoples' rights and in particular: (a) to collect documents, undertake studies and researches on African problems in the field of human and peoples' rights, organise seminars, symposia and conferences, disseminate information, encourage national and local institutions concerned with human and peoples' rights and, should the case arise, give its views or make recommendations to Governments. (b) to formulate and lay down, principles and rules aimed at solving legal problems relating to human and peoples' rights and fundamental freedoms upon which African Governments may base their legislation. (c) co-operate with other African and international institutions concerned with the promotion and protection of human and peoples' rights. 2. Ensure the protection of human and peoples' rights under the conditions laid down in the present Charter. 3. Interpret all the provisions of the present Charter at the request of a State Party, an institution of the OAU or an African Organisation recognised by the OAU. 4. Perform any other tasks which may be entrusted to it by the Assembly of Heads of State and Government.'

[22] ACHPR, Resolution on the Establishment of Committees on Human Rights or Other Similar Organs at National, Regional or Sub-Regional Level, 2nd Annual Report, Annex VIII.

[23] There was brief mention during the 16th session in 1994, but not an in-depth discussion.

[24] It has been an item on the agenda of the African Commission since the 20th session in Mauritius in 1996.

[25] Doc.OS/7(XXI) Add.9, Agenda of the 21st session of the African Commission, Tenth Annual Report of the African Commission on Human and Peoples' Rights, 1996–1997, Annex III, para 7(j). Final Communiqué Twenty-First Ordinary Session of the African Commission on Human and

until the next session when two Commissioners who were also members of NHRIs, Barney Pityana and Rezag-Bara, were tasked to study the issue further and to prepare a draft resolution on the advisory status of NHRIs.[26] The Commissioners' proposals, to offer NHRIs the opportunity to apply for affiliated status with the African Commission[27] was approved and adopted by the Commission at its 24th session in 1998.[28]

This Resolution on the Granting of Observer Status to National Human Rights Institutions in Africa noted the 'importance of the role of national institutions in the promotion and protection of human rights and in creating public awareness in Africa with regard to the institutional defence of human rights'[29] and 'commends the increasing interests shown by African states in establishing and strengthening national institutions for the protection and promotion of human rights based on the principles of independence and pluralism.'[30] Although there is concession to states that each have the 'right . . . to establish, according to its sovereign prerogatives and within the most appropriate legislative framework, a national institution charged with the promotion and protection of human rights according to internationally recognised norms,[31] it does appear to limit participation in the African Commission to those NHRIs which function 'according to internationally recognised norms and standards.'[32]

Affiliated status provides the NHRI with the ability to attend the sessions of the African Commission, participate in relevant discussions and submit proposals to it. In return NHRIs have to submit a report on other activities every two years and assist the Commission in promoting and protecting human rights at the national level. Debate is remarkably open at the African Commission, with equal floor space and participation on all public agenda items being permitted not only for Commissioners, state parties and NGOs with observer status, but now NHRIs. At the African Commission sessions there is now a separate section for NHRIs to sit and in debates they speak after states and before NGOs on all agenda items in the public session, expect for state reporting.

Having adopted this Resolution, the African Commission was then faced with having to examine applications for affiliated status.[33] Some of these were initially

Peoples' Rights, Nouakchott, 15–24 April 1997, at para 14: Resolution on the Granting of Observer Status to National Human Rights Institutions in Africa (1998), ACHPR /Res.31(XXIV)98, as reproduced in App II.

[26] Final Communiqué Twenty-Second Ordinary Session of the African Commission on Human and Peoples' Rights, Banjul, 2–11 November 1997, at para 13.

[27] The Commission's Rules of Procedure could be read as including the possibility of NHRI participation: Rule 72 of the African Commission's Rules of Procedure provides for 'participation of other persons or organisations': 'The Commission may invite any organisation or persons capable of enlightening it to participate in its deliberations without voting rights.'

[28] See above n 25, Resolution on the Granting of Observer Status to National Human Rights Institutions in Africa.

[29] Ibid, preamble to resolution.

[30] Ibid, at para 1.

[31] Ibid, at para 2.

[32] Ibid, at para 4.

[33] The first such applications were from Benin, Nigeria, Sierra Leone and South Africa.

deferred[34] and it is clear that the African Commission struggled with how to establish a procedure to do so. Although one initial suggestion was that a sub-committee should examine the applications before making recommendations to the Commission as a whole, the African Commission repeated the approach that it had created when examining applications for observer status from NGOs.[35] Thus, applications were given to one Commissioner who then, as rapporteur, presented the file to the public session of the Commission and made a recommendation. Other Commissioners are then given the opportunity to comment on the recommendation and grant, postpone or reject affiliated status as a result.

At the time of writing, 19 institutions have gained such status[36] although few make use of it by attending the sessions.[37] Among those that have acquired affiliated status are NHRIs which have not received full accreditation by the ICC.[38]

[34] The 11th Annual Report of the African Commission notes that with respect to its relationship with NHRIs, it deferred applications for affiliated status, although it did not say why, Eleventh Annual Report of the African Charter on Human and Peoples' Rights, 1997–1998, para 36.

[35] Resolution on the Criteria for Granting and Enjoying Observer Status to Non-Governmental Organisations working in the Field of Human Rights with the African Commission on Human and Peoples' Rights.

[36] Comité National des Droits de l'Homme du Cameroun (at 31st session); Comité Sénégalais des Droits de l'Homme (28th Ordinary Session); Commission Nationale des Droits de l'Homme du Rwanda (27th Ordinary Session); Commission Nationale des Droits de l'Homme du Tchad (29th Ordinary Session); Commission Nationale des Droits de l'Homme du Togo (31st Ordinary Session); Commission Nationale des Droits de l'Homme et des Libertés Fondamentales (Niger) (28th Ordinary Session); Conseil National Consultatif pour la Promotion et la Protection des Droits de l'Homme (27th Ordinary Session); Malawi National Human Rights Commission (27th Ordinary Session); National Commission for Democracy and Human Rights Sierra Leone (28th Ordinary Session); National Human Rights Commission of Nigeria (32nd Ordinary Session); National Human rights Commission of Mauritius (31st Ordinary Session); South African Human Rights Commission (31st Ordinary Session); *Conseil National Consultatif de Promotion et de Protection des Droits de l'Homme en Algérie (CNCPPDH)* which had replaced *Observatoire National des Droits de l'Homme de l'Algérie (ONDH)* (33rd Ordinary Session); Permanent Human Rights Commission of Zambia (35th Ordinary Session); Commission Nationale des Droits Humains du Burkina Faso (National Human Rights Commission of Burkina Faso) (35th Ordinary Session); Commission for Human Rights and Good Governance of Tanzania (35th Ordinary Session); The National Human Rights Commission of Kenya (36th Ordinary Session); The Observatoire National des Droits de l'Homme of the Democratic Republic of Congo (36th Ordinary Session); National Human Rights Commission of Ethiopia (40th Ordinary Session); National Human Rights Commission of Uganda (40th Ordinary Session).

[37] At the 32nd session there were 6 NHRIs present, Final Communiqué 32nd Ordinary Session of the African Commission on Human and Peoples' Rights, 17–23 October 2002, Banjul, The Gambia, para 11. At the 33rd session there were 7 NHRIs present, Final Communiqué 33rd Ordinary Session of the African Commission on Human and Peoples' Rights, 1–29 April 2003, Niamey, Niger, para 18. At the 34th session there were 5 NHRIs present, Final Communiqué 34th Ordinary Session of the African Commission on Human and Peoples' Rights, 6–20 November 2003, Banjul, The Gambia, para 11. And 7 at the 36th session, Final Communiqué 36th Ordinary Session of the African Commission on Human and Peoples' Rights, 23 November–7 December 2004, Dakar, Senegal, para 10.

[38] Eg Commission Nationale des Droits de l'Homme du Tchad, which has A(R) status by the ICC; National Commission for Democracy and Human Rights Sierra Leone has not applied for accreditation by the ICC; the Permanent Human Rights Commission of Zambia and the Commission for Human Rights and Good Governance of Tanzania have A(R) status by the ICC; the Commission Nationale des Droits Humains du Burkina Faso has B status by the ICC ; and the Observatoire National des Droits de l'Homme of the Democratic Republic of Congo has not applied for accreditation by the ICC.

One reason suggested why NHRIs have not participated in the sessions nor applied for affiliated status before the African Commission is because of the time taken to process the application. As the Nigerian National Human Rights Commission Executive Secretary stated at the 37th session of the African Commission, if the African Commission were to speed up the process of inviting NHRIs to apply for affiliated status, then more may attend the sessions of the African Commission, feeling more accepted, having achieved such status. The Chair of the African Commission has expressed concern with the limited number of institutions which have applied for such status.[39]

Although there have been instances of those NHRIs which do attend the sessions meeting each other prior to the session, this rarely happens. In only one case has a statement been made by NHRIs outlining collectively what role they would wish to play in the African Commission.[40] Among the recommendations from those at this meeting were that the African Commission should provide them with more information on conferences; that they should meet NGOs to enable them to contribute more effectively to the work of the African Commission, and that the African Commission should ensure better communications with NHRIs and contact them during country visits. It is difficult to tell whether these recommendations were acted upon by the Commission, although there is little evidence to suggest this. One thing that they did succeed in doing, however, was to ensure that NHRIs were able to give a statement at the opening ceremony of the session, on the same basis as was accorded to a representative of states and NGOs.

Beyond the applications for affiliated status, the African Commission's approach to NHRIs has been similar to that of the UN. It has encouraged states to establish such where none exist[41] and during the examination of state reports

[39] See opening speech of Chairperson of the African Commission to the 37th session of the African Commission, on file with author.

[40] At the 30th session of the African Commission in 2001.

[41] It 'invites all the states parties to the Charter, where no national institutions as yet exist for the promotion and protection of human rights, to take appropriate measures to establish such institutions,' ACHPR, Resolution on the Establishment of Committees, above n 22, at para 1. See also: Guidelines on National Periodic Reports, para IV.3(e) 'encourage formation of institutions charged with the responsibility to promote and protect rights guaranteed by the Charter.' In conclusions of a seminar on national implementation of the ACHPR, which the African Commission produced as an Annex of its report 'states party to the Charter are requested to facilitate the establishment and improvement of appropriate national institutions for the promotion and protection of the rights and freedoms guaranteed by the Charter in accordance with Article 26 of the Charter,' Conclusions and Recommendations of the Seminar on the National Implementation of the African Charter on Human and Peoples' Rights in the Internal Legal Systems in Africa, 26–30 October 1992, Banjul, The Gambia, Sixth Annual Activity Report of the African Commission on Human and Peoples' Rights, Annex VIII, para 3(b). In another early resolution on promotion of human rights, the ACHPR also called on states to 'establish national or regional institutes of human and peoples' rights responsible for conducting studies and researches in cooperation with the African Commission on Human and Peoples' Rights and for disseminating the knowledge and information on human and peoples' rights,' Recommendation on Some Modalities for Promoting Human and Peoples' Rights, Second Annual Report of the African Commission on Human and Peoples' Rights, Annex IX, para iii. In its Pretoria Declaration on Economic Social and Cultural Rights, Resolution on Economic, Social and Cultural Rights in Africa, Annex I, states were urged to 'Create

has questioned states on whether they are going to establish such institutions,[42] or to ensure that the powers and remit of existing institutions renders the institution independent and complies with Paris Principles standards.[43] Indeed, states are expressly asked to report on such issues in their Article 62 reports,[44] although it is by no means clear that all have in fact done so. The Special Rapporteurs of the African Commission have contacted NHRIs on their visits to various countries.

The African Commission has also expressed the desire to co-operate with NHRIs[45] and that such institutions are 'essential partners' in implementing the Charter.[46] It sees their role as being to:

independent, impartial and well-resourced national human rights institutions and if they already exist to strengthen their independence and impartiality,' para 11(a)(xx). In a Draft Resolution on Promotional Activities, Fifth Annual Report of the African Commission on Human and Peoples' Rights, Annex X, the Commission noted that 'states parties should established and support national institutions with responsibility for promoting and protecting human and peoples' rights.' Further, 'requests that all states parties should implement Article 26 of the African Charter on Human and Peoples' Rights by establishing national institutions with responsibility for promoting and protecting human and peoples' rights where they do not exist and strengthening all such institutions,' African Commission, Draft Resolution on Promotional Activities, ibid, at para 2. See also: Resolution on the African Commission on Human and Peoples' Rights, Sixth Annual Report of the African Commission on Human and Peoples' Rights, at para.2.

[42] In the concluding observations on Mauritania's state report to the 37th session, the Commission called on the government to 'Take the necessary steps toward the establishment of a National Human Rights Institution functioning according to relevant provisions of the Paris Principles and the resolution of the African Commission governing such institutions,' Draft Concluding Observations on the Periodic Report of the Islamic Republic of Mauritania, on file with author, para 24. For examination of Egypt's state report at the 37th session, the following questions were posed: 'Does Egypt intend to create a National Human Rights Institution in conformity with the wish and principles of the African Commission and of the United Nations system?' In the examination of the state report of Swaziland, the government was asked whether it intended to set up a national human rights institution. The Mauritanian government was asked about whether it intended to set up an independent NHRI, during examination of its state report at the 37th session.

[43] Eg in its report on the Fact Finding Mission to Zimbabwe the African Commission the government was 'urged to establish independent and credible national institutions that monitor and prevent human rights violations, corruptions and maladministration. The Office of the Ombudsman should be reviewed and legislation which accords it the powers envisaged by the Paris Principles adopted. An independent office to receive and investigate complaints against the police should be considered unless the Ombudsman is given additional powers to investigate complaints against the police. Also important is an Independent Electoral Commission. Suspicions are rife that the Electoral Supervisory Commission has been severely compromised. Legislation granting it greater autonomy would add to its prestige and generate public confidence,' African Commission on Human and Peoples' Rights, Zimbabwe. Report of the Fact Finding Mission, June 2002, DOC/OS (XXXIV)/346a, at 31. Questions were also asked about the independence of the Ghanaian NHRI in the examination of its report. In its oral conclusions on the report, the Commission also reiterated the need for the state to strengthen the independence of the NHRI.

[44] Draft Resolution on Promotional Activities, above n 41, at para 5.

[45] In its Mauritius Plan of Action 1996–2001, for example, of the African Commission on Human and Peoples' Rights noted 'in fulfilling its mission, the Commission has to co-operate in promotion and protection of human and peoples' rights, with States parties, international, regional and national institutions as well as non-governmental and inter-governmental organisations in its activities for the promotion and protection of human and peoples' rights in order to attain its objectives in as short a period as possible,' Mauritius Plan of Action, para 47.

[46] Above n 25, Resolution on the Granting of Observer Status to National Human Rights Institutions in Africa (1998).

> serve as a basis for initiatives for human rights in the respective countries, and will help the Commission to disseminate the African Charter and to fulfil its educational mission on human and peoples' rights in general. They may also contribute to protective activities by providing the Commission with information on human rights violations and by assisting the victims of such violations. The Commission intends to set up a cooperation framework between national human rights associations and institutions in order to promote the exchange of information and experience thus assisting them to enhance their efficiency.[47]

Throughout, even in the earlier references to NHRIs, the African Commission has stressed the need for compliance with the Paris Principles or equivalent.[48]

Although the African Commission has recommended the establishment of a focal point for NHRIs within the Secretariat of the African Commission[49] and there is considerable potential for NHRIs to engage with the Commission, there appears to be little enthusiasm to develop this in practice. Despite encouraging states to establish such institutions, and encouraging their attendance, the African Commission has done little to engage NHRIs more in its work or in ensuring that those who do work with it comply with the Paris Principles.[50] Neither has it amended its Rules of Procedure to reflect the position of these new observers.[51] Contrary to the position at the UN, where participation is more difficult, and yet NHRIs are eager for greater involvement, at the African Commission's open meetings, NHRIs have expressed little interest in exploiting this to its full potential. NHRIs may not see any benefit in spending resources on attending these meetings. Despite recognising the need for involvement at the regional and international levels, NHRIs have expressed disappointment in the meetings of the African Commission. It is apparent that much of this disappointment and unwillingness to participate further in the meetings of the Commission stems from the manner in which the sessions are held, including frustrations over the lack of a clear programme and agenda and not feeling part of the network of those who attend these events.[52] Those that have obtained affiliated status have done so for various reasons, including that members of the

[47] Mauritius Plan of Action, above n 45, at paras 65, 67–68.

[48] African Commission, Resolution on the Establishment of Committees on Human Rights or Other Similar Organs at National, Regional or Sub-Regional Level, above n 22, at para 2.

[49] Report of the Retreat of Members of the African Commission on Human and Peoples' Rights (ACHPR) facilitated by the Office of the High Commissioner for Human Rights (OHCHR), African Union Conference Centre, Addis Ababa, Ethiopia, 24–26 September 2003, http://www.nhri.net/pdf/ACHPR-Retreat-Report-Final.pdf, 9.

[50] Human Rights Watch, *Protectors or Pretenders? Government Human Rights Commissions in Africa* (New York, Human Rights Watch, 2001) 68. The African Commission has been considering a workshop on 'the African Commission and national Structures for the promotion and protection of human and peoples' rights.' See African Commission on Human and Peoples' Rights, Sixth Annual Report of the African Commission on Human and Peoples' Rights, at para D. At the time of writing, this workshop had yet to be held.

[51] Although the Rules of Procedure are currently undergoing review by the Working Group on Issues Relating to the Work of the African Commission. It is likely that such revisions will take account of the role of NHRIs.

[52] Interview with member of NHRI, 7 April 2006.

NHRI itself sat on the African Commission and this was therefore a way of formalising collaboration.[53] However, some NHRIs have expressed the feeling that they 'don't have a meaningful relationship with the African Commission. It has a lot to offer but . . . there is no on-going dialogue.'[54] Members of NHRIs feel that the African Commission should be seeking information from them, in a more proactive way, on what the situation is in the respective countries, or at least ensuring some direct communication with them.[55]

In January 2004 the Protocol to the African Charter on Human and Peoples' Rights Establishing an African Court on Human and Peoples' Rights came into force.[56] After considerable delay caused by discussions on whether and how to merge this court with the other AU judicial body,[57] the African Court of Justice, the AU agreed to start the operation of the Human and Peoples' Rights Court pending any future merger.[58] As a result, in January 2006, eleven judges were elected to the Court[59] and they have begun to consider their Rules of Procedure. Although NHRIs are not mentioned in the Court, it is worth considering at least whether they will play any role at all in it. Article 5 of the Protocol provides that the following can submit cases to the Court: the African Commission, states which have lodged a complaint with the Commission, states against whom a case has been lodged with the Commission, and states whose citizens are victims of violations, and African intergovernmental organisations. It does, however, provide that NGOs with observer status before the African Commission, and individuals, can 'institute cases directly before' the Court if the state has made a prior statement of acceptance, under Article 34(6) of the Charter. So far only one two states have done so.[60] If one sees NHRIs as outside the state structure, this leaves no scope for the submission of cases by NHRIs, unless they indirectly submit a case to the African Commission and this is then passed to the Court. Although the relationship between the African Commission and the Court has still to be determined, there is the potential that NHRIs could lobby for a role for themselves while the Rules of Procedure are being determined. Furthermore, although the Protocol establishing the Court which will merge the African Court on Human and Peoples' Rights and the African Court of Justice is yet to be finalised, there is already some recognition of the role of NHRIs within this proposed

[53] Eg the former Chair of the South African Human Rights Commission, Barney Pityana, was also a member of the African Commission on Human and Peoples' Rights at the time.

[54] Interview with member of NHRI, 7 April 2006.

[55] Ibid.

[56] Protocol to the African Charter on Human and Peoples' Rights Establishing an African Court on Human and Peoples' Rights, 1998, entered into force on 25 January 2004.

[57] See: Decision on the Seats of the African Union, Assembly/AU/Dec.45(III).

[58] Decision on the Merger of the African Court on Human and Peoples' Rights and the Court of Justice of the African Union, Assembly/AU/Dec.83 (V).

[59] Decision on the Election of the Judges of the African Court on Human and Peoples' Rights, Assembly/AU/Dec.100 (VI).

[60] Burkina Faso and Mali.

body. Article 31 sets out a list of 'other entities eligible to submit cases to the Court' and among them are 'African National Human Rights Institutions'.[61]

SUB-REGIONAL LEVEL

More recently, NHRIs have also begun to be noticed at the sub-regional level where a number of initiatives have been taken. In particular, member states of ECOWAS have an obligation to create NHRIs and the Commission of ECOWAS has to take measures to strengthen the capacity of NHRIs and create a network.[62] NHRIs should submit 'systematically to the Executive Secretary any report of human rights violations observed on its territory'.[63] An Expert Planning Workshop and brainstorming meeting was held, to this end, in July 2006 in Accra.

FORA CREATED BY AFRICAN NHRIs THEMSELVES

Beyond involvement in the regional organisations, African NHRIs have also created forums among themselves for collaboration and co-ordination of activities. As in other regions of the world, so the African NHRIs have grouped themselves together and hold conferences, the results of which have been Declarations outlining their collective approach.[64] These regional meetings have in their resolutions urged an increased role for NHRIs in the African Commission on Human and Peoples' Rights[65] and their resolutions have been transmitted to this body as well as to the UNHCHR and the International Coordinating Committee.[66]

[61] Draft Protocol on the Statute of the African Court of Justice and Human Rights, May 2006, EX.CL/211 (VIII) Rev.1, Annex II, Article 31(e).

[62] ECOWAS Protocol on Democracy and Good Governance, Executive Secretary, Dakar, December 2001, PROTOCOL A/SP1/12/01, Article 35.

[63] Ibid, Article 35(2).

[64] Eg First Conference of African National Human Rights Institutions (ANHRIs), Yaoundé, Cameroon, 5–7 February 1996; Second Conference of African National Human Rights Institutions, 1–3 July 1998, Durban, South Africa; Third Conference of African National Human Rights Institutions, Lomé, Togo, 14–16 March 2001; Fourth Conference of African National Human Rights Institutions, Kampala, Uganda, 14–16 August 2002; Fifth Conference of African National Human Rights Institutions, Abuja, 8–10 November 2005.

[65] The Durban conference also 'urges the African Commission for human and Peoples' Rights in its next session to adopt an appropriate resolution on the effective participation of national institutions in the work of the Commission,' Durban Declaration, para 14. The Third Conference also urged African NHRIS to apply for affiliated status from the African Commission on Human and Peoples' Rights, Third Conference of African National Human Rights Institutions Held in Lomé, Togo, 14–16 March 2001, Lomé Declaration, ibid, para VII.1.

[66] Ibid, at para X.1. It then called on the CCANI to transmit the Declaration to the UN Human Rights Commission, the African Commission on Human and Peoples' Rights, Ministerial Conference on Human Rights in Africa, and the CCANI to submit a report to the Third Conference of African NHRIs on progress in implementation of the Declaration, Durban Declaration, above n 64, at paras 22 and 23.

It was at these conferences where the idea of establishing a regional formal structure for African NHRIs was raised and put in motion. At the First Conference of African National Human Rights Institutions (ANHRIs) in Yaoundé, Cameroon, held 5–7 February 1996, it was decided to create a Coordinating Committee of African NHRIs (CCANI) to work with the ICC and the UN Centre for Human Rights to,

> ensure follow up of the proceedings of the First Conference of African National Institutions held in Yaoundé; facilitate the activities of National Institutions for mutual strengthening in the discharge of their respective mission; envisage other African meetings every two years alternating with international conferences; negotiate a proper representative status on the African Commission on Human and Peoples' Rights, and support the efforts of the International Coordinating Committee in the search for National Institutions with the United Nations bodies dealing with human rights issues.[67]

The CCANI is composed of eleven countries from the five regions of Africa. Whereas the African NHRI group as a whole can include institutions that are not formally accredited by the ICC, members of the CCANI have to be from accredited institutions. The members of CCANI are the fourteen NHRI accredited by the ICC that are in compliance with the Paris Principles. Members are appointed for two years, which can be renewed once, and they are representatives of their institutions and regions.[68] The CCANI is supposed to meet at least once a year and where necessary during meetings of the ICC, the UN Human Rights Commission, or African Commission on Human and Peoples' Rights.[69]

At the fourth conference of African NHRIs in 2002 the Rules of Procedure for CCANI were adopted and a decision was taken to establish a permanent secretariat for African NHRIs[70] to be hosted by South Africa for the first three years.[71] The main role of the secretariat was to 'provide capacity-building support to African National Human Rights Institutions (ANHRIs), in order to enable them to carry out their mandate to defend and strengthen human rights and to inform and educate the public about their human rights.'[72] It intended to operate by organising training and meetings and events around sharing practices and ideas; giving advice to states which are thinking of setting up commissions; giving support to African NHRIs and the Coordinating Committee; disseminating information and research, and following up from Coordinating Committee and International Coordinating Committee decisions. It was hoped that the South African Human Rights Commission would provide the Secretariat with resources for its operation. However, there were difficulties in getting this secre-

[67] Yaoundé Declaration, above n 64, at para 17.

[68] Rules of Procedure of the Coordinating Committee of African National Institutions for the Promotion and Protection of Human Rights, Arts 5 and 6.

[69] Ibid, Art 15(a).

[70] Kampala Declaration, above n 64, preamble.

[71] Ibid, at para 5(i).

[72] http://www.sahrc.org.za/index5.htm

tariat operating, and despite the existence of a website,[73] it has not been a visible presence and has so far not provided a meaningful service to the CCANI.[74] Although there appears to be a close relationship between the Secretariat and the South African Human Rights Commission, in practice this has not had any implications as the Secretariat barely functioned. The Secretariat will now be hosted by the Kenya Human Rights Commission, but stressing that the Secretariat 'would not be under the direction of the NHRI per se but remain accountable to the CCANHRI as a whole.'[75] Any Secretariat plans have to be approved by a steering committee of the Coordinating Committee, in consultation with other Coordinating Committee members.[76]

CONCLUSION

The trend, in the later resolutions of the UN Human Rights Commission, was to open the way for participation of NHRIs. In the meantime, the African Commission has always welcomed the involvement of NHRIs in its sessions and work, but in practice little has developed. The approach to NHRIs at these levels has therefore ranged from caution, to welcome indifference. In both these arenas, and perhaps explaining why there is inconsistency in approach within and between them, there are a number of issues that have not been fully considered but which should be central to the future participation of NHRIs. First, participation at the international and regional levels has depended mainly on whether one can claim to be a state, the primary actor, or a non-state actor, where additional mechanisms might be used. Applying this dichotomy to NHRIs, as chapter 5 will illustrate, is not straightforward. Secondly, when looking for justifications as to why any non-state actor might legitimately participate at the international or regional levels, one of the key issues in respect of NHRIs is their independence. However, as chapter 5 will discuss, this notion has not been clearly defined and tensions apparent at the domestic level have been played out internationally and regionally. Lastly, the extent of participation that NHRIs should be accorded at the international and regional levels has so far been determined by NHRIs. Even where UN and regional bodies have established their own mechanisms of participation for these institutions, this has

[73] Its website (http://www.sahrc.org.za/index5.htm) is hosted by the South African Human Rights Commission.

[74] An executive director for the African NHRI Secretariat has still not yet been appointed due to lack of funds, Meeting of the Coordinating Committee of African National Human Rights Institutions (CCANHRI) and its Secretariat, 12 April 2005, Geneva, Switzerland, www.nrhi.net, at para 5.

[75] Ibid, at para 6.

[76] At the time of writing, the Steering Committee of CCANI were: Nigeria (Chair), as First Vice Chair: Rwanda; as Second Vice Chairs: Uganda and Kenya. Elected as representatives to the ICC are Malawi, Morocco, Nigeria and Rwanda. The Regional Group's representative to the Sub-Committee on Accreditation of the ICC is Nigeria.

looked towards the accreditation accorded by NHRIs to each other. The extent to which the international accreditation procedures are appropriate regulatory bodies and whether NHRI should be accountable at this level, are also important considerations which will be examined in chapter 6.

5

NHRIs as State or Non-State Actors

AS THE PREVIOUS chapters illustrate, there is no consistent approach to the involvement of National Human Rights Institutions (NHRIs) whether one is examining the UN Charter or treaty bodies, or the African mechanisms. Although NHRIs have been involved, what participation has been permitted has not been based on any serious consideration of the role and place of NHRIs generally. One of the reasons why this is the case, it is submitted, is because of the ambiguity of NHRIs as state or non-state actors in a legal system which is premised on the idea that participation of various entities will fall into one or either category.

NHRIs AS STATE OR NON-STATE ACTORS

The traditional view sees states at the centre of international law[1] and participation at the international level has depended often, therefore, on whether the entity can claim it is a state.

To what extent, therefore, are NHRIs part of the state and should be treated as such? On the one hand, NHRIs can be seen as part of the state and the state is delegating some of their powers and authorities to it.[2] If NHRIs are part of the state, then this does not raise problems of participation, as they simply form part of the state delegation to any meetings. Yet seeing NHRIs as part of the state apparatus does not fit with the notion of them as 'independent' institutions.

Over the years the involvement of other actors on the international plane has led to a discussion on the status of these 'non-state actors.'[3] This label has been

[1] See C Warbrick, 'States and Recognition in International Law' in M Evans, *International Law* (Oxford, Oxford University Press, 2003) 205–67.

[2] This can have an impact in terms of the dominance of the state in international law, C Schreuer, 'The Waning of the Sovereign State: Towards a New Paradigm for International Law?' (1993) 4 *EJIL* 447–71.

[3] P Alston, *Non-State Actors and Human Rights* (Oxford University Press, 2005); A Clapham, *Human Rights in the Private Sphere* (Oxford, Oxford University Press, 1993); RA Higgott, G Underhill and A Bieler (eds), *Non-State Actors and Authority in the Global System* (Routledge, London, 2000).

applied to a variety of entities including individuals,[4] NGOs,[5] multinational corporations,[6] international organisations, terrorist groups and paramilitary organisations.[7]

What is encompassed within the definition of a non-state actor, however, is not settled, although there have been various attempts to define it. Alston suggests one of the 'most comprehensive'[8] is one which,

> includes all organizations: largely or entirely autonomous from central government funding and control: emanating from civil society, or from the market economy, or from political impulses beyond state control and direction; operating or participating in networks which extend across the boundaries of two or more states–thus engaging in 'transnational' relations, linking political systems, economies, societies; acting in ways which affect political outcomes, either within or one more states or within international institutions–either purposefully or semi-purposefully, either as their primary objective or as one aspect of their activities.[9]

For those such as non-governmental organisations (NGOs) ('') the label of non-state actor may be easier to apply (even if in reality it may not always be correct). For NHRIs, however, which are presumed to have been created in some official way through legislation or constitution, the question of whether they are state or non-state actors is more problematic. In some instances, because of the manner in which they are established, despite the requirement that they operate independently, they are seen as part of the state apparatus.[10] On the other hand, precisely because NHRIs should be acting independently of government, it is seen important that they occupy a separate space and be viewed as non-state actors in their own right.

[4] R McCorquodale, 'The Individual and the International Legal System', in M Evans, *International Law*, 299–325; PK Menon, 'The International Personality of Individuals in International Law: A Broadening of the Traditional Doctrine' (1992) 1 *Journal of Transnational Law and Policy* 151; R Lord, 'The Liability of Non-State Actors for Torture in Violation of International Humanitarian Law: An Assessment of the Jurisprudence of the International Criminal Tribunal for the Former Yugoslavia' (2003) *Melbourne Journal of International Law* 112.

[5] Eg MT Kamminga, 'The Evolving Status of NGOs under International Law: A Threat to the Inter-State System?' in P Alston, *Non-State Actors and Human Rights* 93–112; H Cullen and K Morrow, 'International Civil Society in International Law: The Growth of NGO Participation' (2001) 1 *Non-State Actors in International Law* 7; D Shelton, 'The Participation of Nongovernmental Organizations in International Judicial Proceedings' (1994) 88 *AJIL* 611.

[6] S Ratner, 'Corporations and Human Rights: A Theory of Legal Responsibility' (2001) 11 *Yale Law Journal* 443; M Addo, *Human Rights Standards and the Responsibility of Transnational Corporations*, (The Hague, Kluwer Law International, 1999); P Muchlinski, *Multinational Enterprises and the Law* (London, Blackwell, 1999).

[7] W Schabas, 'Theoretical and International Framework: Punishment of Non-State Actors in Non-International Armed Conflict' (2003) 26 *Fordham Journal of International Law* 907.

[8] P Alston, 'The "Not-a-Cat" Syndrome: Can the International Human Rights Regime Accommodation Non-State Actors?' in P Alston, *Non-State Actors and Human Rights* 3–36, at 15–16.

[9] Ibid, at 15–16.

[10] Added to this, as Willetts notes, are difficulties when the notion of the state, so central to international human rights law, is wrongly equated with the apparatus of government, P Willetts, 'Transnational Actors and International Organizations in Global Politics' in JB Baylis and S Smith (eds), *The Globalisation of World Politics* (Oxford and New York, Oxford University Press, 2nd edn, 2001) 356–83.

The division of actors into two opposing camps, state and non-state, is not that straightforward and has implications for how those non-state actors are dealt with:

> this insistence upon defining all actors in terms of what they are not combines impeccable purism in terms of traditional international legal analysis with an unparalleled capacity to marginalize a significant part of the international human rights regime from the most vital challenges confronting global governance at the dawn of the twenty-first century.[11]

Indeed, many have pointed out the increasing challenges to state exclusivity in international law with the involvement of a variety of other actors bringing with it concerns that democracy may be compromised as a result.[12] International institutions could step into this void by ensuring some accountability for the activities of these other entities.

Yet this distinction between state and non-state has been developed, as Alston argues, not because of 'language inadequacies' but more to underline the idea that the state is the central figure in international human rights law: 'Accordingly, for the purposes of international legal discourse—the language of human rights—those other entities can only be identified in terms of their relationship to the state.'[13]

An alternative may be to see responsibility as attributed to both the state and the NHRI. This 'double attribution' has been recognised in a number of places in relation to responsibility of the individual and the state: 'individual responsibility does not necessarily mean that the state is atomised and that the state could negate its own responsibility by having responsibility shifted towards individual state organs–state responsibility can exist next to individual responsibility.'[14] It is possible, therefore, that the international organs can view the operation and effectiveness of an NHRI as a matter for both the state and the NHRI itself to explain.

SUBJECTS AND OBJECTS OF INTERNATIONAL LAW

Because international law traditionally only applies obligations and rights to the subjects of international law,[15] if one can argue that non-state actors are also

[11] Alston, above n 8, at 3.

[12] PR Trimble, 'Globalization, International Institutions and the Erosion of National Sovereignty and Democracy' (1997) 95(6) *Michigan Law Review* 1944–69, at 1946–47; D Bodansky, 'The Legitimacy of International Governance: A Coming Challenge for International Environmental Law?' (1999) 93 *American Journal of International Law* 596–624. See also: T Franck, *Fairness in International Law and Institutions* (Oxford, Clarendon Press, 1995).

[13] Alston, above n 8, at 3–4.

[14] A Nollkaemper, 'Concurrence between Individual Responsibility and State Responsibility in International Law' (2003) 52 *ICLQ* 615–40, at 618–21.

[15] A Reinisch, 'The Changing International Legal Framework for Dealing with Non-State Actors', in P Alston, *Non-State Actors and Human Rights* 37–89, at 70.

subjects of international law, then one can impose rights and obligations on them.

The well-known debate around who are subjects, and conversely objects of international law, has been applied to these non-state actors such as NGOs, multinational corporations and others, but so far not applied to NHRIs. Who has international legal personality and who is a subject of international law has, traditionally, been defined by asking who has 'the capacity to bear rights and obligations under international law.'[16] However, some of the discussion on NGOs and the difficulties they have had to face in this regard is particularly pertinent to the case of NHRIs especially as 'this creation of a binary opposition of "subject" v "object" has become part of the definition of international legal personality.'[17]

As has been noted in the Reparations for Injuries Case by the International Court of Justice, who is a subject of international law can vary depending on what is required at any one time: 'the subjects of law in any legal system are not necessarily identical in their nature or in the extent of their rights, and their nature depends on the needs of the community. Throughout its history, the development of international law has been influenced by the requirements of international life, and the progressive increase in the collective activities of states has already given rise to instances of action upon the international plane by certain entities which are not states.'[18]

To what extent do NHRIs have rights and obligations in international human rights law? In one sense human rights law documents now address obligations towards non-state actors anyway. For example, the Universal Declaration of Human Rights mentions the duty of 'every individual and every organ of society . . . shall strive by teaching and education to promote respect.for these rights and freedoms'[19] In addition, the treaty bodies of the UN and the regional bodies have obligations specifically towards non-state actors. In its Concluding Observations on Cameroon's state report, at its 31st session, the Committee Against Torture urged the state to take certain measures to end torture, but also directed the National Committee on Human Rights and Freedoms to 'pay more frequent visits to all places of detention.'[20] Similarly, the African Commission has called upon NHRIs to 'follow up on relevant resolutions and recommendations concerning the strengthening of national institutions'[21] and in one Resolution set out separate obligations for

[16] B Cheng, 'Introduction to Subjects of International Law' in M Bedjaoui (ed), *International Law: Achievements and Prospects* (Paris, UNESCO, 1991) 23, at 38.

[17] McCorquodale, above n 4, at 301.

[18] Reparation for Injuries, Advisory Opinion, ICJ Rep. 1949, 174, at 178.

[19] Preamble, UDHR, see Reinisch, above n 14, at 71.

[20] 31st session, CAT/C/CR/31/6, para 8(a).

[21] Commission on Human Rights, Effective Functioning of Human Rights mechanisms: National Institutions and Regional Arrangements, E/CN.4/2005/L.92/Rev.1, 19 April 2005, para 18.

states, NGOs and NHRIs.[22] NHRIs have also given statements at opening ceremonies of the African Commission, sharing the platform with states and NGOs.[23]

It is clear, therefore, that even though the UN and regional bodies have acknowledged that NHRIs should be accorded a different status from states,[24] obligations have been addressed to them as non-state actors in their own right.[25] In addition, as was discussed in chapter 2, the active participation of NHRIs in the drafting of treaties suggests that they have become more significant players on the international field.[26]

Is this sufficient, however, to assert that NHRIs are also subjects of international law? This question of whether an entity is a subject or otherwise of international law is of little relevance to practice, besides being rather circular:

> why would we want to show that non-state actors are subjects of international law? To demonstrate that they may be direct addresses of human rights obligations. How do we try to show that they are subjects of international law? By asserting that they are direct addressees of human rights obligations under international law. Truly, the suspicion that the whole matter of international legal personality forms a vast intellectual prison and that the 'whole nation of subjects and objects has no credible reality and [. . .] no functioning purpose' is sometimes hard to suppress.[27]

[22] In the Pretoria Declaration on Economic, Social and Cultural Rights, it noted specific obligations for NHRIs: '*National Human Rights Institutions should* (i) Undertake studies, monitor and report on economic, social and cultural rights; (ii) scrutinise existing laws and administrative acts and make submissions to Parliament on bills relating to economic, social and cultural rights; (iii) Publish and distribute their reports on economic, social and cultural rights; (iv) Establish regional networks /coalitions and involve NGOs in these coalitions; (v) Apply for affiliate status with the African Commission, if they have not done so; (vi) Raise awareness on economic, social and cultural rights among particular groups such as the public service, the judiciary, the private sector and the labour movement and encourage the Government to integrate human rights in the school curricula; (vii) Examine complaints of infringements of economic, social and cultural rights and make recommendations on redress, and where possible file cases before national courts; (viii) Conduct follow up activities in the implementation of recommendations of international treaty bodies and publicize their reports, especially on economic, social and cultural rights; (ix) Advocate for States to ratify the Protocol of the African Human Rights Court and to make the declaration allowing NGOs and individuals to file cases; (x) Advocate for the African Human Rights Court to be established without further delay,' African Commission on Human and Peoples' Rights, Pretoria Declaration on Economic, Social and Cultural Rights, para 11.

[23] Eg at its opening sessions the African Commission always hears not only from the Chair of the Commission, a representative of states, a representative of NGOs, but now also a representative of NHRIs. See, eg at the 33rd session of the African Commission on 15 May 2003, the Chairperson of the Commission Nationale des Droits de l'Homme et des Libertés Fondamentales du Niger made a statement on behalf of NHRIs at the opening ceremony, see Final Communiqué 33rd Ordinary Session of the African Commission on Human and Peoples' Rights, 15–29 May 2003, Banjul, The Gambia.

[24] Eg at the 26th session of the African Commission when discussing how to deal with NHRIs, one Commissioner affirmed that NHRIs should be accorded a different status from that of states and NGOs and that the term 'affiliated status' reflected this. See R Murray, 'Report of the 1999 Sessions of the African Commission on Human and Peoples' Rights' (2001) 22 *Human Rights Law Journal* 172–98.

[25] Reinisch, above n 15, at 72.

[26] ECOSOC in its decision 2004/14, Comprehensive and Integral International Convention on Protection and Promotion of the Rights and Dignity of Persons with Disabilities.

[27] Reinisch, above n 15, at 72.

This makes sense and what may be more relevant, in terms of the practice of international law and their impact upon it, is not so much whether an entity is a subject or object, but rather who participates in the international and regional arenas.[28]

NHRIs AS PARTICIPANTS

Whether one considers NHRIs or NGOs, the extent of their participation may differ from entity to entity. Rather than seeing the international and regional arenas as composed of state and non-state actors, it is more realistic to look at it in terms of 'a multi-layered reality consisting of a variety of authoritative structures. Under this functionalist approach what matters is not the formal status of a participant . . . but its actual or preferable exercize of functions.'[29] It is clear that other actors, beyond states, have had a role in drafting of treaties, for example, or adjudication.[30]

So far many NHRIs have used this state/non-state dichotomy to their advantage, preferring in some instances to be part of a government delegation, yet in others to act separately, when deciding which tactic would be more effective. It is important, however, that there is greater clarity over their role and position.

If NHRIs are part of the state there would seem to be no problem in ensuring their participation in practice. They simply form part of the state delegation. Indeed, this is the approach adopted by several NHRIs at the international treaty body level and the African Commission.[31] However, if one sees NHRIs as non-state actors, one then has to decide the extent to which they can participate in international and regional forums, and the procedures for determining such. While precedents have been set by NGOs,[32] individuals,[33] national liberation movements, and they are not treated the same as states,[34] these approaches are

[28] 'The whole notion of "subjects" and "objects" has no credible reality, and, in my view, no functional purpose. We have erected an intellectual prison of our own choosing and then declared it to be an unalterable constraint,' R Higgins, *Problems and Process: International Law and How We Use It* (Oxford, Oxford University Press, 1994) 49.

[29] Schreuer, above n 2, at 453.

[30] Ibid, at 464.

[31] 'For example, the Comísion Nacional de los Derechos Humanos (CNDH) represents the Mexican government at the UN Working Group on Enforced and Involuntary Disappearances, a role that has been welcomed by the Working Group itself. Yet, this seems like a confusion of roles: the task of the CNDH, after all, should be to hold its government to account over disappearances, not to occupy its seat when it is forced to answer international inquiries,' International Council on Human Rights Policy, *Performance and Legitimacy: National Human Rights Institutions* (Geneva, ICHPR, 2000) 100.

[32] ECOSOC Resolution 1996/31 which provides for NGOs to obtain consultative status.

[33] Through the submission of communications, for example, to regional and international bodies, eg Optional Protocol to the UN ICCPR.

[34] Despite NGOs having such status in the UN Human Rights Commission, they are not given the same status as states: ECOSOC Resolution 1996/31 states 'the arrangements for consultation should not be such as to accord to nongovernmental organisations the same rights of participation as are accorded to States not members of the Council and to the specialised agencies . . .,' at para 18.

not necessarily consistent and depend on the particular actor under consideration. If NHRIs were simply NGOs they could use the procedures available to the latter, but NHRIs differ from NGOs in their semi-offcial status. It is possible, however, for NHRIs to draw on the experiences of NGOs and adapt them to fit their own situation. For example, through creating a procedure of participating in international and regional forums, NHRIs can come to be seen as legitimate actors on the international plane.[35] This is the case even if on paper the ability to participate is limited.[36] They could have a considerable impact on international law, going beyond what might have been envisaged as being possible from the formal consultative status they have been granted. With their semi-official status and potentially closer relationship with governmental political players, NHRIs have greater opportunity for being involved in many of the activities that NGOs have found themselves in, such as drafting treaties,[37] by being mentioned in treaties as having a role to ensure compliance of the state with its obligations,[38] and in bringing cases before international and regional bodies.[39]

As the number of actors on the international and regional planes increases, however, there is a concern that rather than increase the democratic nature of the systems, there is a reduction in the space for interaction. As, for example, the number of NGOs, NHRIs and other actors who want to make statements and participate in these meetings rises, so the possibility of a meaningful exchange between them and the UN or African Commission may decrease[40]:

> The challenge will be to find a model, on the one hand, allowing for substantial contribution of NGOs and non-state actors in general, while, on the other, taking into account the necessary limits of participation of non-state actors. The debate promises to be lengthy and difficult, not only in light of the current dichotomy between open and closed societies, but also because the issue is not confined to a specific legal regime, but goes to the very fundaments of how international law works, and who its actors and, in the end, its legal subjects are.[41]

[35] 'Nevertheless, once NGOs are inside the system they gain a distinct type of legitimacy which may be crucially important to an NGO's success because of their distinctive international ontology which is often at variance with many national governments. Thus, participation in an international forum with the opportunity to challenge their sovereign governments–something that they may not be able to do domestically–may be quite a coup,' C Breen, 'Rationalising the Work of UN Human Rights Bodies or Reducing the Input of NGOs? The Changing Role of Human Rights NGOs at the United Nations' (2005) 5 *Non-State Actors and International Law* 101–26, at 105.

[36] Eg r 34(2) of the UN CRC Rules of Procedure, see ibid, at 110.

[37] Eg in the Convention on the Rights of the Child, ibid, at 106–08.

[38] Eg Convention on the Protection of the Rights of All Migrant Workers and Members of their Families, Art 74(6); Art 45 UN CRC), ibid, at 109–10.

[39] H Cullen and K Morrow, 'International Civil Society in International Law: The Growth of NGO Participation' (2001) 1 *Non-State Actors and International Law* 7–39.

[40] JD Aston, 'The United Nations Committee on Non-Governmental Organizations: Guarding the Entrance to a Politically Divided House' (2001) 12(5) *EJIL* 943–62.

[41] Ibid, at 962.

There is equally a concern that as international meetings and sessions become more crowded, there is a drive for greater efficiency which in turn could lead to limits being imposed on the number or extent of non-state actor participation. As part of discussions on how to streamline and make more efficient the work of the UN human rights bodies, so participation of NGOs have also been an issue. In discussions on the increased efficiency of the UN Human Rights Commission this has been the case, with discussions on re-evaluating the role of NGOs in its work.[42] The result of discussions on this issue has meant the cutting back of speaking rights of some NGOs at the Commission.[43] This has led to concerns that NGOs are being sidelined in the Commission under the guise of greater efficiency.[44] This is even more so where states attempt to occupy the space given to non-state actors such as NGOs and NHRIs themselves. For example, governments, under the guise of their NHRIs have attacked NGOs.[45] There is also some evidence that the interests of donors in providing NHRIs with funding may deprive NGOs of such support.[46]

While NHRIs are relatively new to the international and regional fields, and their status is still very much open to debate, they have similarly already started to make a not insignificant contribution to the development of international law. However, just because in formal terms they may not be seen as subjects of international law, does not mean that their influence is not felt in practice.[47] As with many non-state actors, the theory does not reflect the practice[48]: 'it therefore follows that the role, status and implications of NGOs in global governance would be better understood if looked at within a broader context that understands current trends in international politics rather than what legal texts say.'[49]

One area where NHRIs could play a particularly influential role is at earlier stages of the development of international standards, for example, in defining the terms used and giving information to those involved in the formal processes.[50] If NHRIs are able to manage political relationships by acting as

[42] Breen, above n 35, at 118–19.

[43] Ibid, at 125–26.

[44] Ibid.

[45] Eg at the 61st session of the UN Human Rights Commission, the Rwandan Commission Nationale des Droits de la Personne challenged 'baseless allegations' by some NGOs that they had not been allowed to function freely, Press Release. National Human Rights Institutions Outline their Work to Commission on Human Rights, 13 April 2005, www.unhchr.ch.

[46] Human Rights Watch, *Protectors or Pretenders? Government Human Rights Commissions in Africa* (New York, Human Rights Watch, 2001) 77.

[47] 'NGOs have become or are increasingly becoming legitimate actors contrary to traditional theories of international law and international relations.' One reason may be because there are an increasing number of 'sites of authority' and 'sources of legitimation,' meaning that state consent is not the only source of legitimacy, B Maragia, 'Almost There: Another way of Conceptualizing and Explaining NGOs Quest for Legitimacy in Global Politics' (2002) 2 *Non-State Actors and International Law* 301–32, at 301.

[48] Ibid, at 304–05.

[49] Ibid, at 318.

[50] JA Scholte, 'Civil Society and Democracy in Global Governance' (2002) 8 *Global Governance* 281–304.

information providers and by acquiring expertise in particular areas and providing an alternative source of information to policy makers, they have the potential to be influential.[51] While, as we saw in chapter 2, they may also be seen as legitimate participants because they can offer another source of information beyond states and NGOs, NHRIs may often not have the expertise to play a lobbying role. Yet how they use the arenas available to them, even if limited, can have more influence than their formal status implies: 'Successful participation . . . takes a certain level of political ingeniousness or sophistication.'[52]

In order to influence the international system, other non-state actors may have to be involved over a longer time, even if their involvement has not been recognised formally.[53] In contrast, NHRIs are new to the international and regional arenas and are still finding their space and trying to work out their role. On the one hand, NHRIs operate within the confines of international law and practice and have to use traditional rules to justify their involvement and participation. In so doing, they can create a certain personality for themselves. Having gone through an appropriate process the actor can then claim legitimacy for its involvement in these arenas.[54] However, one can argue that just as the participation of NGOs has illustrated a shift away from the state as the central authority, to 'multiple sources of legitimacy,' so NHRIs are also not required to go 'through traditional processes of legitimation to be deemed legal persons or legitimate actors.'[55]

If NHRIs are to argue for participation in international and regional arenas and have a role in creating international norms, then surely it is justifiable that they should be subject to the same standards of accountability as are applied to other actors on the international plane: 'participation in global norm creation comes with responsibility and accountability on the part of those who make them.'[56]

Of course, by focusing on states as the only actors on the international plane, it is argued that the role of non-state entitles, including NGOs, has been downplayed from what it actually may be in reality.[57] To acknowledge the role of NGOs or non-state actors in the system and the importance they play, can imply that states are not the only entitles that can influence international law.[58]

[51] D Berlin, 'The Key to Green Power–Explaining NGO Influence in Global Environmental Governance Structure,' prepared for NISA-NOPSA Conference, Reykjavik, 11–13 August 2005, Workshop Globalization as Individualization and Destabilization.

[52] Ibid, at 11. He talks about the organisation's 'informational capacity (to produce relevant fact contributions to the process), another is the tactical ingeniousness (knowing whom to approach when and how), yet another being the communicative proficiency (capacity to frame issues in a winning manner). Together this parcel of resources makes up an organization's political skill,' at 12.

[53] L Jordan and P Van Tuijl, 'Political Responsibility in Transnational NGO Advocacy' (2000) 28(12) *World Development* 2051–65, at 2054.

[54] Ibid, at 312.

[55] Ibid, at 307.

[56] Ibid, at 313–14.

[57] Ibid, at 323.

[58] Ibid, at 324.

CONCLUSION

The extent of participation of actors in arenas such as the Human Rights Commission, treaty bodies and the African Commission on Human and Peoples' Rights depends on whether they are defined as state or non-state actors. To be part of the state could ensure easy access for NHRIs to these forums, yet this is difficult to square with the supposed independence of such institutions. On the other hand, this requires NHRIs to argue for their participation on the basis of being a non-state actor, the privilege to do so being determined through a political process often dependent on state approval.[59] As this chapter has illustrated, there are sufficient examples of non-state actors participating for NHRIs to argue for a similar approach to be applied to them. However, to place NHRIs in a state/non-state camp ignores their status as semi-official independent bodies.

Because the African and UN bodies have by and large conducted their business on a state/non-state model, the result has been a hesitancy, caution and inconsistency in how to deal with NHRIs. What is needed is a more detailed analysis of the role of participants and the extent that each should be involved on that basis. There are several issues that are important to bear in mind. First, it is essential that careful consideration is given as to the space that NHRIs occupy and how this should be reflected in their participation in the UN and regional meetings. Moving beyond procedures which apply simply to states or non-state actors is essential if there is a recognition of the role of the NHRI in society. Without proper consideration of the procedure for determining their role at this level, the treatment of NHRIs runs the risk of following that adopted towards NGOs: they could be potentially significantly influential in practice, but without this being monitored by a mechanism that ensures they are accountable for their actions at these levels. If the international system is to recognise that it has become the multi-actor setting which it is in practice, then in order to ensure that the position is not abused by the variety of actors themselves or states using the vague status of these actors for their own means, then there needs to be a debate on the role that non-state actors such as NHRIs play at this level, and how this role can be adequately reflected and monitored through a procedure of recognition.

[59] NGOs gain consultative status to ECOSOC, as provided for under Art 71 of the UN Charter on the recommendation of the UN's Committee on Non-Governmental Organizations, a standing committee of ECOSOC. This is made more specific by Resolution ECOSOC 1996/31, UN Doc.E/1996/31, 25 July 1996. But the criteria on which they apply, the political manipulations of states and the conduct of this Committee has been greatly criticised, Aston, above n 40, at 945. 'The wider the scale and geographical focus in which an NGO operates, the larger the coalition of member states in the Committee opposing the application tends to become. In this respect, the fox is guarding the hen-house,' at 950.

6

Ensuring the Accountability of NHRIs. What Role for the International and Regional Bodies?

JUST AS THE issue of 'good governance' has been applied to state behaviour, so it has been rolled out to apply to other actors at the international level.[1] Good governance has been developed as a concept which applies the rule of law to international organisations and procedures and the processes of decision-making.[2] It has been defined as:

> a condition whereby a responsibility acquired through election; appointment or delegation is discharged in an effective, transparent, and accountable manner while bad governance is associated with maladministration in the discharge of responsibility. Good governance entails the existence of efficient and accountable institutions-executive, judicial, administrative, economic, corporate-and entrenched rules that promote development, protects human rights, respects the rule of law, and ensures that people are free to participate in, and be heard on, decisions that affect their lives.[3]

So should good governance principles also apply to NHRIs? On the one hand, it is arguable that,

> the international human rights regime's aspiration to ensure the accountability of all major actors will be severely compromised in the years ahead if it does not succeed in devising a considerably more effective framework than currently exists in order to take adequate account of the roles played by some non-state actors. In practice, if not in theory, too many of them currently escape the net cast by international human rights norms and institutional arrangements.[4]

[1] A Reinisch, 'The Changing International Legal Framework for Dealing with Non-State Actors' in P Alston, *Non-State Actors and Human Rights* (Oxford, Oxford University Press, 2005) 37–89, at 49–50. See also: P McAuslan, 'Good Governance and Aid in Africa' (1996) 40(2) *Journal of African Law* 168–82.

[2] J Hatchard, M Ndulo and P Slinn, *Comparative Constitutionalism and Good Governance in the Commonwealth: An Eastern and Southern African Perspective* (Cambridge, Cambridge University Press, 2004); J de Wilde, 'Flagging Democracy' (2004) 17(2) *International Journal for the Semiotics of Law* 211.

[3] United Nations Economic Commission for Africa, 'Information Resources on Africa' www.uneca.org.

[4] AP Alston, 'The "Not-a-Cat" Syndrome: Can the International Human Rights Regime Accommodate Non-State Actors?' in P Alston, *Non-State Actors and Human Rights* 3–36, at 6.

Is there, however, something different from NHRIs that means they should not be subject to such standards?[5] Accountability in terms of states poses less difficulty. Yet if one sees the international arena as now allowing for the participation of a variety of actors, then who is accountable and for what is more problematic.[6] If, however, the system is to be 'ethically and legally coherent,' then it is imperative that we 'should seek to regulate those actors who, in a political, economic and cultural sense, are autonomous and therefore act significantly at the international level.'[7]

An analysis of comments from the UN, African institutions and NHRIs themselves suggest that one of the roles that the UN and international and regional forums play with respect to NHRIs is in respect of their accountability. This is particularly the case when considering the role of the ICC and the accreditation process. The aim of this chapter is to examine the role of the international and regional systems in terms of providing accountability of the NHRI.

WHAT IS ACCOUNTABILITY?

The concept of accountability has been the subject of considerable debate and there are a variety of approaches that can be taken.[8] In one respect it starts from 'face to face relationship of individuals.'[9] It can simply require that the 'performance of a service is no more than the sum of the actions performed, and if these are done conscientiously and competently, then all is well with the service as a whole.'[10] However, even this is premised on some basic understanding of what is an appropriate level of performance which in some ways may not be easy to agree.[11] Going beyond this, accountability could encompass a variety of political and managerial issues.[12] Accountability often refers to the responsibility of government or actors to whom government has delegated certain

[5] R Lehr-Lehnardt, 'NGO Legitimacy: Reassessing Democracy, Accountability and Transparency' (2005) Cornell Law School LLM Paper Series, Paper 6, http://lsr.nellco.org/cornell/lps/clacp/6, at 2.

[6] C Harding, 'Statist Assumptions, Normative Individualism and New Forms of Personality: Evolving a Philosophy of International Law for the Twenty First Century' (2001) 1 *Non-State Actors and International Law* 107–125, at 121.

[7] Ibid, at 122–23.

[8] As the House of Lords noted 'accountability is a generic term, the precise definition of which depends on the circumstances, including the relationship between the interested party to the regulator. In practice, there are multiple accountabilities,' House of Lords Select Committee on the Constitution, *The Regulatory State: Ensuring its Accountability*, 6th Report of Session 2003–2004, HL Paper 68-I, 6 May 2004, para 48.

[9] C Scott, 'Accountability in the Regulatory State' (2000) 27(1) *Journal of Law and Society* 38–60, at 40.

[10] P Day and R Klein, *Accountabilities. Five Public Services* (London, Tavistock Publications, 1987) 236.

[11] Ibid, at 4–5.

[12] Ibid, at 27.

functions. The issue of how accountability can be extended to other actors, however, is increasingly relevant.[13]

If one takes accountability as 'the duty to give account for one's actions to some other person or body,'[14] then applying the notion of accountability to NHRIs poses a number of difficulties. First, NHRIs, as is the case often with service providers, may see their role differently from others.[15] As a result, applying 'value-for-money' approaches can be seen as inappropriate for NHRIs whose aim is to promote and protect human rights.[16] So with some service providers who are operating in a context in which other factors and the role of other institutions also play a part as to whether results are achieved, namely, for example, whether human rights are indeed protected, focusing on performance of one particular institution to produce results may not be appropriate.

Furthermore, if a key feature advocated of NHRIs is that they should be independent, then does any system of accountability imply control that may limit that independence? Therefore:

> In broad terms, watchdogs should be accountable only for matters of performance . . . rather than for the merits of their recommendations, policies or goals. In most cases, accountability should be after the fact, rather than the sort of pre-accountability that involves seeking consent prior to a course of action, through a business plan or structuring the action by prescribing the rules.[17]

On the other hand one could see NHRIs as experts who obtain their authority not by the fact that it is delegated to them from government, but 'from their own special knowledge and skills.'[18] In this sense, should they be accountable for the advice that they give?[19]

Despite these difficult issues, accountability of NHRIs is becoming increasingly relevant, not only domestically, but at the international level. Here the accreditation process adopted by the International Coordinating Committee of National Human Rights Institutions (ICC) and other bodies implies that NHRIs are accountable and by enabling NHRIs to participate in the international and regional arenas, accreditation at these levels may impact on the legitimacy of the institution domestically: 'it may be that wider participation in international jurisdictions' proceedings promotes their legitimacy, at least among those seeking to participate.'[20]

[13] Scott, above n 9, at 48.

[14] Ibid, at 40.

[15] Eg service providers may see 'accountability, answerability, or responsibility as being direct to the "community" at large, rather than following the lines of constitutional accountability,' Day and Klein, above n 10, at 229.

[16] Ibid, at 246.

[17] N Smith, 'Policing the Constitution' [1997] *Public Law* 234–44, at 237–38. See for discussion of independence and accountability in the context of the judiciary, K Malleson, *The New Judiciary. The Effects of Expansion and Activism* (Dartmouth, Ashgate, 1999).

[18] Day and Klein, above n 10, at 16.

[19] Malleson, above n 17, at 86.

[20] L Bartholomeusz, 'The *Amicus Curiae* before International Courts and Tribunals' (2005) 5 *Non-State Actors and International Law* 209–86, at 283.

WHO IS ACCOUNTABLE?

Given this, it is essential then to consider who is accountable, to whom are they accountable, and for what are they accountable.[21] As noted in chapter 5, NHRIs do not sit easily within a state/non-state dichotomy. A key element of their effectiveness and the reasons behind a drive for them to be established is their potential ability to operate independently from government, yet at the same time being established in a formal manner that presupposes government commitment to them. In terms of the accountability of the NHRI itself, the difficulty with NHRIs is that it is not often clear whether it is the government which should be accountable for the NHRI or the NHRI itself. State obligations in international human rights law may require it to establish an NHRI that is independent and adequately resourced and funded, and on which it should be questioned as a result. Indeed, this is the approach adopted by UN and regional bodies. For example, the UN treaty bodies have stressed the obligations of the state first to establish an independent body[22] and then to ensure that it not only does not interfere with its work, but supports it and implements its recommendations.

The main approach of the UN bodies and African regional institutions is to regulate the activities of NHRIs through the notion of state responsibility[23] and increasingly making international norms part of the domestic legal order.[24] On the one hand, state responsibility for those to whom it has delegated authority may not cause any particular difficulties and one could see the NHRI has occupying this role. On the other, if the NHRI is seen as a separate institution in its own right, to what extent should the state be responsible for its activities? State responsibility for non-state actors could be implied from the obligations of the state to go beyond 'respect' for human rights but also that it 'ensure' them.[25] So where activities of non-state actors lead to a violation of human rights law, the state can be held indirectly responsible as part of its obligation to 'ensure' those rights.[26] Thus, in a case against Chad, the African Commission held that, under the obligations in Article 1 of the Charter for states to 'recognise the rights, duties and freedoms in this Charter and shall undertake to adopt legislative or

[21] Scott, above n 9, at 41.

[22] Eg in its Concluding Observations on Sudan's initial report to the ICESCR, the Committee on Economic Social and Cultural Rights 'welcomes the establishment of the Sudan national Committee for the Eradication of Harmful Practices,' Committee on Economic, Social and Cultural Rights, Concluding Observations of the Committee on Economic, Social and Cultural Rights: Sudan, 1 September 2000, E/C.12/1/Add.48, para 10. It went on to recommend that 'in light of the recent establishment of committees addressing specific human rights issues, the Committee encourages the state party to establish an independent national human rights institution, in accordance with the 1991 Paris Principles,' at para 31.

[23] See 2001 Articles on the Responsibility of States for Internationally Wrongful Acts, UN Doc.A/56/10 (2001), as approved by the General Assembly, Res.56/83 (2001). Alston, above n 4, at 24.

[24] Reinisch, above n 1, at 53.

[25] Ibid, at 79.

[26] Ibid.

other measures to give effect to them,' 'if a state neglects to ensure the rights in the African Charter, this can constitute a violation, even if the state or its agents are not the immediate cause of the violation.'[27] Under the government's 'responsibility to secure the safety and liberty of its citizens, and to conduct investigations into murders. Chad is therefore responsible for the violations of the African Charter.'[28] As Reinisch notes, 'the policy rationale underlying such "vicarious" or "subsidiary" liability is clear: to increase pressure on states by continuing to hold them responsible for "out-sourced" or "delegated" activity in order to make sure that they have a direct interest in regulating the behaviour of non-state actors to whom they have transferred state tasks.'[29]

The UN and regional bodies have also implied that state obligations towards NHRIs extend beyond this and in doing so, start to enter into questions about how the NHRI itself is carrying out its work. For example, when examining Kenya's initial report to the UN Committee on the Rights of the Child (UNCRC) the Committee noted the establishment of a Standing Committee on Human Rights in 1996 but was,

> concerned that insufficient resources (financial and human) have been allocated for the effective functioning of the SCHR. The Committee notes with concern that the SCHR has no specific responsibilities with regard to children and that the SCHR is not easily accessible to children. The Committee encourages the State party to allocate adequate financial and human resources to the Standing Committee on Human Rights (SCHR) to ensure its effective functioning. The Committee further suggests that the State party should consider reviewing the status of the Committee and establishing an independent national human rights institution in accordance with the Paris Principles (General Assembly resolution 48/134) which would be competent to monitor and evaluate progress in the implementation of the Convention at the national level and, if appropriate, at the local level and to receive and investigate complaints of violations of child rights in a child-friendly manner, and to address them effectively. Meanwhile, the State party should take effective measures to ensure that the SCHR is easily accessible and child-sensitive in dealing with complaints of violations of the rights of children and in providing remedies for such violations in all regions of the country. The Committee further suggests that the State party initiate an awareness raising campaign about the SCHR and to facilitate its effective use by children. The Committee encourages the establishment of a focal point on children within the SCHR to monitor child rights. Finally, the Committee suggests that the State party consult further with OHCHR and seek technical assistance from UNICEF, among others.[30]

Should it be the state which is responsible for ensuring that the NHRI is 'accessible and child sensitive,' that there is sufficient awareness about its work

[27] Communication 75/92, *Commission Nationale des Droits de l'Homme et des Libertés v Chad*, Ninth Annual Activity Report of the African Commission on Human and Peoples' Rights, 1995–1996, AHG/207 (XXXII), Annex VIII, para 20.

[28] Ibid, para 22.

[29] Reinisch, above n 1, at 81.

[30] Committee on the Rights of the Child, Concluding Observations of the Committee on the Rights of the Child: Kenya, 7 November 2001, CRC/C/15/Add.160, paras 16–17.

and dictating how it is structured internally with the establishment of a focal point, or should this be within the responsibility of an independent institution itself? How that institution carries out its activities, particularly if it is supposed to operate separately from government, should be seen as falling under its own competence, rather than that of the government. If the institution is truly not subject to the influence or control of government, then how it chooses to operate, structure itself internally, raise awareness of its work, spend its money and prioritise will not be something over which the government has control. Furthermore, as research has indicated, the independence and the effectiveness of an NHRI is not always dependent on the state, but on the institution itself, as well as other stakeholders in society.[31] Measuring the effectiveness of an NHRI and how it performs is not solely dependent on the manner in which the NHRI itself carries out its mandate or spends its funding. It also depends on a variety of other factors including how it is perceived in the eyes of other stakeholders in society, the extent of the resources and powers it was given when established, and the political and social and constitutional context in which it finds itself.[32]

Scott's distinction between 'upwards accountability' where this is to a higher authority, 'horizontal accountability,' to 'parallel institutions,' or 'downwards accountability,' to 'lower level' bodies, may be useful in this regard.[33] There is thus a distinction between issues that are within the control of government, over which it should be answerable, such as defining the mandate of the institution, its establishment and creation, and those issues which should be within the remit of the institution itself, such as how it carries out its activities. One might presume, therefore, that the more independent and separate the institution is from government, the more the institution itself should be answerable for its activities. Conversely, the less independent the institution is, the more the government should be accountable. This is not a division that has been applied clearly by the UN or African bodies, however. This may in part be due to the fact that international and regional bodies can only address their recommendations in many procedures to the state itself (for example, state reporting, individual communication, etc) rather than to other actors.

If the NHRI is to be personally responsible for certain activities, there are a number of ways of doing so such as through the use of voluntary codes of conduct[34] and translating international norms into domestic law.[35] The extent

[31] S Livingstone and R Murray, *Evaluating the Effectiveness of National Human Rights Institutions. The Northern Ireland Human Rights Commission and Comparisons with South Africa*, 2005.

[32] Ibid.

[33] Scott, above n 9, at 42.

[34] See: United Nations Draft International Code of Conduct on Transnational Corporations, 23 ILM (1984) 626; OECD, Guidelines for Multinational Enterprises, 21 June 1976, 15 ILM (1976) 969; UN Sub-Commission on the Promotion and Protection of Human Rights, Norms on the Responsibilities of Transnational Corporations and Other Business Enterprises with Regard to Human Rights, E/CN.4/Sub.2/2003/12/Rev.2.

[35] Reinisch, above n 1, at 37–89.

to which NHRIs should themselves voluntarily subscribe to the Paris Principles and other standards is worth considering.[36] Certainly, codes of conduct have also been used in relation to other non-state actors such as international organisations,[37] as well as NGOs, sometimes in response to criticism directed towards them and to protect their own credibility.[38]

FOR WHAT ARE THEY ACCOUNTABLE?

One would imagine that whereas NHRI cannot be held accountable for the conditions under which they are established and the manner of the appointment of their members, for example, it could be argued that they should be accountable for how they perform their mandate. NHRIs have a broader aim to promote and protect human rights within their jurisdiction. But it is very difficult to measure the impact of what an NHRI does on whether human rights have been improved in any given context given the host of other factors at play.[39] If, for example, one took a simple 'value for money' approach to accountability, as has been noted in respect of other public service providers, there is, 'considerable suspicion . . . as somehow being incompatible with services dedicated to the public good and perhaps also threatening qualitative and professional objectives.'[40]

So should NHRIs simply be accountable for carrying out their activities, namely, 'that the performance of a service is no more than the sum of the actions performed, and if these are done conscientiously and competently'?[41] Surely an NHRI should be accountable for how it spends its money at the very least? There is no coherent approach to this issue at the international level and the only benchmarks against which NHRIs are assessed are their compliance with the Paris Principles. As seen above, this is often addressed at the state rather than the NHRI itself and how it may choose to carry out its functions and spend its money. For example, in its Concluding Observations on Ghana at its 62nd session, the Committee on the Elimination of Racial Discrimination questioned the state on the case load of the Commission on Human Rights and Administrative Justice:

> notes that out of a total of 9265 complaints heard by the Commission in 2000, the CHRAJ only dealt with fewer than five complaints directly relating to alleged racial

[36] Ibid, at 44–45.

[37] Eg Observance by United nations Forces of International Humanitarian Law, United Nations, Secretary-General's bulletin, ST/SGB/1999/13, 6 August 1999, 36 ILM (1999) 1656. Reinisch, above n 1 at 46–48.

[38] Eg Codes of Conduct of the International Red Cross (Principles of Codes of Conduct for the International Red Cross and Red Crescent Movement and NGOs in Disaster Response Programmes), Reinisch, above n 1, at 49.

[39] M Green, 'What We Talk About When We Talk About Indicators: Current Approaches to Human Rights Measurement' (2001) 23(4) *Human Rights Quarterly* 1062–97.

[40] Day and Klein, above n 10, at 235.

[41] Ibid, at 236.

> discrimination. According to the state party, the majority of complaints received by the Commission were cases of religious discrimination which, because religion in Ghana is often related to ethnicity, could be classified in some cases, as indirect racial discrimination. The Committee would like to receive more detailed information on this matter, as well as statistical information relating to the number of complaints having a bearing on racial discrimination, and the action taken by the Commission.[42]

Similarly, in its Concluding Observations on Uganda at its 62nd session, the Committee on the Elimination of Racial Discrimination 'requests that in its next periodic report, the state party provide additional information on the specific activities and achievements of the Commission, particularly with regard to implementation of the Convention.'[43] This goes beyond simply requiring the government to make sure the Commission is independent and actually questioning on how the Commission is doing its work.[44] Some of the UN treaty bodies have gone further and directed what they think the NHRI should be doing, calling on the state to ensure that this is implemented. So in the case of the NHRI in Senegal, the Committee on Economic, Social and Cultural Rights encouraged the state to 'ensure that national human rights institutions do not concentrate solely on civil and political rights, but accord equal weight and attention to economic, social and cultural rights.'[45] NHRIs themselves do not necessarily feel the need to justify their performance at the international or regional levels, but more see their role as providing information on what the government has done in their countries, or what they have themselves been doing.[46]

[42] 62nd session, CERD/C/62/CO/4, 2 June 2003, para 16.

[43] Ibid, para 17.

[44] See also in its Concluding Observations on Malawi at its 63rd session, the Committee on the Elimination of Racial Discrimination was 'concerned that the budgetary constraints facing the Malawi Human Rights Commission may limit its effectiveness. The Committee recommends that the state party including information on this issue in its next periodic report. It also recommends the information on the functions and activities of the Malawi Human Rights Commission be disseminated both in English and in Chichewa,' 63rd session, CERD/C/63/CO/12, 10 December 2003, para 12.

[45] 26th session, E/C.12/1/Add.62, 24 September 2001, para 37.

[46] Eg Statement by Justice Elton Singini, SC, Law Commissioner/Human Rights Commissioner for Malawi to the 61st Session of the United Nations Commission on Human Rights, Geneva, Switzerland, April 2005, at 1. Statement to the 61st Ordinary Session of the United Nations Commission on Human Rights, Presented by the Deputy Chairperson of the South African Human Rights Commission, Geneva, 13 April 2005, www.nhri.net. A similar approach was taken by the Tunisian Comité Superieur des Droits de l'Homme et des Libertés Fondamentales de Tunisie, 61eme Session de la Commission des Droits de l'Homme, Déclaration Présentée par Dr Najoua Miladi au Titre du point 18 'Fonctionnement efficace des Mécanismes des Protection des Droits de l'Homme,' Genève, 13 avril 2005, www.nhri.net. Statement from the Kenya National Commission on Human Rights, Presented at the 61st Session of the United Nations Commission on Human Rights, by Maina Kiai, Chairman, Kenya National Commission on Human Rights, April 2005, Geneva, www.nhri.net. Press Release. National Human Rights Institutions Outline their Work to Commission on Human Rights, 13 April 2005, www.unhchr.ch

TO WHOM ARE NHRIs ACCOUNTABLE?

The second difficulty arises in determining to whom the NHRI is accountable: 'Traditional approaches to accountability have a very narrow notion of accountability giving only those with formal authority over an individual or organisation the right to hold them to account.'[47] For many NHRIs this would be government. But this inevitably raises a difficult paradox, whereby the aim is to ensure an independent NHRI that is not answerable to government but that can operate separately from it.

Accountability of NGOs also raises similar difficulties and it has been suggested that they may be accountable not only to their employees, volunteers, members, donors and intended beneficiaries.[48] Given that most NHRIs, particularly in Africa, are supported by external donors, whatever their level of independence from government,[49] should NHRIs be accountable to those who provide them with financial support? This raises some concerns if NHRIs are to operate without undue influence or control from others. Taking into account the role that NHRIs should play and their interaction and reliance on a variety of actors in society, one more acceptable approach could be to see accountability as being to a variety of stakeholders in society and in this sense could be 'direct to the "community" at large,'[50] or 'any group or individuals who can affect or is affected by . . . an organisation.'[51] This notion of 'stakeholder accountability' means that 'stakeholders are encouraged to be involved at all stages of an organisation's decision making in order to ensure that the organisation is responsible for its actions.'[52]

Again, this raises some tensions. For example, an organisation like an NHRI may find it difficult to please all of its stakeholders and can become too bureaucratic and expensive. It may require them to serve different needs which may not match those for which they have been established or for which they have powers. In addition, requiring the NHRI to be answerable to different sectors could impact on its independence.

So should NHRIs be accountable at the international level? There are a number of attractions with this approach. It avoids difficulties of stakeholders imposing demands, and avoids problems of making an NHRI answerable to government. One can see authority on regulation spread among a number of actors and organisations and examine how all of these actors interact with each

[47] H Kovach, C Neligan and S Burall, *Power Without Accountability* (One World Trust, 2002/2003) at 3.

[48] Lehr-Lehnardt, above n 5, at 28.

[49] Human Rights Watch, *Protectors or Pretenders? Government Human Rights Commissions in Africa* (New York, Human Rights Watch, 2001) 77.

[50] Day and Klein, above n 10, at 229.

[51] Kovach, Neligan and Burall, above n 47, at 3.

[52] Ibid, at 3.

other.[53] This fits particularly well with a system which is pluralist, as one could now argue the international legal arena is: 'Pluralist approaches to law and regulation have particular application to global governance. International regulatory norms, formal and informal, are developed in multiple sites, public and non-governmental.'[54] Even if one envisages the responsibility for NHRIs as being part of state obligations, 'the dispersal of regulatory authority creates relationships of interdependence negotiated between the actors within the regulatory space.'[55] This leads us to a 'form of extended accountability' which looks more at interdependence rather than independence.[56]

This mode, however, presumes involvement of a number of actors in determining the accountability of an NHRI. As has been seen, at present this accountability is decided by NHRIs themselves through a process of self-regulation. This is despite NHRIs suggesting that they should perhaps not be subject to any standards at all: 'we need to hold ourselves accountable to ourselves.'[57]

HOW ARE NHRIs ACCOUNTABLE? PROCESS OF ACCOUNTABILITY

As outlined in chapter 2, the extent to which NHRIs can participate, be accredited and gain legitimacy at the international and regional levels relies often on a process of regulation. Decisions as to which NHRIs may participate at the level of the UN and to a lesser extent at the African Commission on Human and Peoples' Rights, are dealt with by the ICC, a body of NHRIs applying the UN General Assembly Paris Principles to determine accreditation and participation. Membership of the ICC is only open to 'national institutions which comply with the Paris Principles.'[58] Those wishing to be members have to apply to the chair of the ICC and send its founding documentation, its organisational structure, its annual report, and 'a detailed statement that it complies with the Paris Principles or, alternatively, an outline of any respects in which it does not so comply and any proposals to ensure compliance.'[59]

There is an extensive list of information that NHRIs have to submit to the Sub-Committee on Accreditation.[60] This includes information on the mandate and structure,[61] accountability,[62] protection and promotion functions,[63]

[53] Scott, above n 9, at 331.

[54] Ibid, at 333.

[55] Ibid, at 337.

[56] Ibid, at 338.

[57] Comment by Maina Kiai, Chair of the Kenya National Human Rights Commission, 17th session of the ICC, April 2006.

[58] Rules of Procedure of the ICC, r 3(a).

[59] Rules of Procedure of the ICC, r 3(c). Rules of Procedure of the ICC Sub-Committee on Accreditation, as adopted by the members of the International Coordinating Committee at its 15th session, Seoul, Republic of Korea, 14 September 2004, para 3.3.

[60] Accreditation of National Institutions, www.nhri.net.

[61] 'Explain the relationship between your mandate and structure and your founding document,' ibid.

[62] 'Indicate line of accountability and how institution is accountable,' ibid.

[63] 'Explain where defined and what those functions are, if no, give reasons,' ibid.

responsibility,[64] independence,[65] method of operation,[66] additional criteria for institutions with quasi-judicial competence,[67] general information,[68] jurisdiction[69] and scope.[70] The Sub-Committee will not consider applications from new institutions until they have completed the first year of their activity and are able to submit an annual activity report to it.[71]

Much of the information required by the ICC, however, may be considered as not being within the ability of the NHRI to determine. Thus, how it is established, what functions it has, who its members are, for example, are issues determined by those establishing it, not the NHRI itself. Yet it is the NHRI which must advocate and lobby for its accreditation by the ICC, not the state.

Documentation has to be sent at least two months before the ICC meeting[72] and it is then passed on to members of the Sub-Committee.[73] The Sub-Committee meets prior to and after the meeting of the yearly meeting of the ICC in order to consider any applications and make its recommendations to the ICC.[74] This is a private meeting at which only members of the Sub-Committee and OHCHR are able to be present.[75] There have been recent instances where members of NHRIs have been asked to provide oral statements before the Accreditation Sub-Committee, although the Committee was keen to state that although this was not a sustainable practice due to the time it would take to hear each application, there was a need to ensure consistency of approach when examining applications.[76]

NHRIs can be classified by the Sub-Committee as falling within four categories:

[64] 'Whether it has responsibility to submit opinions, reports, promote consistency, encourage ratification, contribute to UN reporting independently of government, conduct research, increase public awareness of human rights, etc., and to give supporting documentation of these and examples of programmes,' ibid.

[65] 'Guaranteed by pluralist composition, appointment and dismissal process established by law with fixed term and renewable, financial autonomy derived from stable adequate funding, legal and operational autonomy through separate legislation, infrastructure and resources,' ibid.

[66] 'Is the institution free to meet regularly and as required, review any matter within own jurisdiction . . . hear any person and obtain any information related to a matter . . . ; make public its findings and recommendations; establish local and regional sections; maintain consultation with other bodies (eg NGOs) when carrying out its functions,' ibid.

[67] 'Is the institution competent to potentially hear individual complaints; potentially seek settlement through conciliation or binding decisions with confidentiality?; inform the complainant of their rights and remedies and ensure the process is accessible? Potentially make recommendations to competent authorities, make enforceable decisions or refer to specialised tribunal?' ibid.

[68] Eg type of institution (ombudsman, commission, other), ibid.

[69] ie domestic, private, public, international, ibid.

[70] ie general, thematic, ibid.

[71] Report and Recommendations of the Sub-Committee on Accreditation, International Coordinating Committee of National Human Rights Institutions for the Promotion and Protection of Human Rights, 16th Session, Geneva, 14–15 April 2005.

[72] Rules of Procedure of the ICC Sub-Committee on Accreditation, above n 59, at para 3.4.

[73] Ibid, at para 3.6.

[74] Ibid, at para 4.1.

[75] Ibid, at para 4.2.

[76] 17th session of the ICC, April 2006.

A: Compliance with Paris Principles
A(R): Accreditation with Reservation—'granted where insufficient documentation is submitted to confer A status'.
B: 'not fully compliant with the Paris Principles or insufficient information provided to make a determination (observer status)'.
C: 'Non-compliant with the Paris Principles.'[77]

The Chair of the Sub-Committee gives a report with reasons to members of the ICC 'for their decision.'[78] 'The ICC Chairperson will indicate in the report of the meeting decisions taken by ICC members with regards to applications for accreditation. The Chairperson of the ICC will inform applicant institutions of the decisions taken and their rationale by ICC members.'[79] Once the Sub-Committee has made its decision, the NHRI can ask for clarification of this decision 'in order to ensure transparency in the Committee's decision-making.'[80] Discussion of the report of the Sub-Committee by the ICC can mean, therefore, that the plenary body can amend or refuse to adopt the report if they are not happy with its contents. The result is that there are inevitably NHRIs which are not Paris Principles compliant and can influence the accreditation of others.

Any decision which is adverse to a particular institution with respect to membership has to be discussed with it.[81] If membership is declined then, if the ICC consents, the NHRI can attend meetings as an observer and can reapply for membership.[82] Any changes to the NHRI which may affect Paris Principles should be made known to the Chairperson of the ICC by the institution which will put it to the Accreditation Sub-Committee. The membership can be reviewed.[83]

These issues raise a further difficulty as at the level of the ICC, it is the NHRI itself that is lobbying for its approval, on issues that are arguably not within its control, such as how its members are appointed, the situation in the country and what its geographical reach is. Yet, it is the NHRIs which have to persuade the ICC to accredit them, when one might expect that it would be the state. For the ICC to interact with the state could raise difficult issues of independence, but is an avenue the ICC itself has used, for example, by requiring further information on a particular NHRI not only to be sought from the NHRI itself, but from the government authorities.[84]

[77] UN OHCHR, Member States Meeting Geneva, 28–29 June 2004. National Institutions Activities, January–June 2004, 16 June 2004, 9. These are replicated in Rules of Procedure of the ICC Sub-Committee on Accreditation, above n 59, at para 5.

[78] Rules of Procedure of the ICC Sub-Committee on Accreditation, above n 59, at para 6.1.

[79] Ibid, at paras 6.2 and 6.3.

[80] Report and Recommendations of the Sub-Committee on Accreditation, above n 71.

[81] Rules of Procedure of the ICC, r 3(d), (e).

[82] Rules of Procedure of the ICC, r 3(f).

[83] Rules of Procedure of the ICC, r 3(g).

[84] At the 17th session of the ICC, further information was sought on a number of institutions which were not granted full accreditation by the ICC, Report and Recommendations of the Sub-Committee on Accreditation, above n 71.

Although on the face of it, one would think that this process provides a certain amount of regulation over the activities of NHRIs, in practice, the extent to which the ICC exercises effective regulatory control over NHRIs is debatable. Certainly it has become more robust in recent years and the ICC has stated that it 'stands fully committed to continue its work to strengthen the accreditation procedures for NHRI—both in terms of assessing the formal legal framework and the actual performance of NHRIs.'[85] So it has withheld full status from the Commission Nationale des Droits Humains of Burkina Faso, as it was,

> of the opinion that the institution is not in full compliance with the Paris Principles. . . . as the level of funding from the government appears to be inadequate. It is, however, noted that although the institution's budget is appended to that of the Ministry responsible for human rights, this is not in itself considered to be incompatible with the Paris Principles. The institution needs to demonstrate that it has adequate financial independence. Further, due to its lack of financial autonomy, the institution does not have its own premises or permanent staff. Further, the Secretary-General of the CNDH is appointed by the Prime Minister. The institution needs to demonstrate that appointment of the Secretary-General has taken place with sufficient consultation and transparency.'[86]

NHRIs have also not been accredited if they have failed to provide the full and proper documentation, as was the case with the DRC's Observatoire National des Droits de l'Homme[87] and Tanzania's Commission for Human Rights and Good Governance. [88]

Despite this more detailed consideration and although the National Institutions Unit (NI Unit) of the OHCHR has provided much needed secretarial support to the ICC, there are still no funds available to the ICC itself to make visits to institutions to assess them.[89] In addition, as the above procedures illustrate, it is not clear exactly who is being assessed: the state or the NHRI, through

[85] Statement by Morten Kjaerum, Director, Danish Institute for Human Rights. Chairperson International Coordinating Committee of National Institutions for the Promotion and Protection of Human Rights (ICC), at the Sixty-First Session of the Commission on Human Rights, Geneva, 13 April 2005, at 1.

[86] It was granted A(R) status by the ICC, Report and Recommendations of the Sub-Committee on Accreditation, International Coordinating Committee of National Human Rights Institutions for the Promotion and Protection of Human Rights, 16th Session, Geneva, 14–15 April 2005.

[87] This was because 'a fully activity report was not submitted as part of the application.' 'It is recommended that it be granted temporary A(R) status,' Report and Recommendations of the Sub-Committee on Accreditation, above n 71.

[88] It had made its first application in 2003 and been granted A(R) 'for lack of documentation specifically the most recent Annual Report.' In April 2005 the Sub-Committee made no change to this status 'no change has been made in terms of the institution's 2003 application. The lifting of the reserve is conditional upon the submission of an annual report for 2003 which are to be approved by Parliament.' In addition, 'there is no indication of the recent activity of the institution in an annual report for 2003,' Report and Recommendations of the Sub-Committee on Accreditation, ibid.

[89] Enhancing the Participation of National Human Rights Institutions in the Work of the Commission on Human Rights and its Subsidiary Bodies, Report of the Secretary-General, 19 January 2005, E/CN.4/2005/107, para 14.

a process which calls primarily on the NHRI to justify its compliance with the Paris Principles.

When considering the role of the African conferences and African Coordinating Committee of African National Human Rights Institutions (CCANI), a lack of regulation is even more apparent. The Rules of Procedure of the Coordinating Committee of African National Institutions for the Promotion and Protection of Human Rights[90] note in Article 2 that the African Group is to be composed of all African NHRIs whether or not theyare accredited by the ICC. However, this is contradicted by Article 7 of the Rules of Procedure which states that 'if in the majority opinion of the Committee, an institution does not comply with the Paris Principles or is not discharging its functions as a member of the Committee, an ad hoc Committee shall be established to investigate the matter.' This committee will then make a report within 90 days on whether membership should be suspended or other steps taken and can make a recommendation to the ICC to revisit its accreditation. What exactly 'not discharging its functions' means is not clear and there have been no instances of this being applied. There is some minimal regulation in that only NHRIs which are accredited by the ICC can sit on the Committee, or have the right to vote.[91]

All African NHRIs are required to submit 'their annual reports,' namely the annual report prepared for domestic purposes, to the Chairperson and Secretariat of the CCANI every two years.[92] It is not clear how many NHRIs have sent this report to the CCANI and certainly, the CCANI has done nothing substantive with them.

It is also problematic that the African NHRI conferences focus more on developing good practice but have not so far berated members or excluded them for lack of compliance with the Paris Principles. Neither the African NHRI conferences nor CCANI have issued any statement expressing concern over a situation in a particular country, for example, choosing instead to focus on standard setting or supporting each other. As a result, enabling weak or ineffective institutions to participate at these levels does grant them a certain degree of legitimacy but without any accountability.[93] This is done, as well, without outside scrutiny or input, whether this is from NGOs, activists, or other international organisations, the meetings being held primarily among members of NHRIs themselves.[94]

The picture is not much better when one considers the African Commission on Human and Peoples' Rights, despite its formal procedure of NHRIs having to apply for affiliated status. There is, then, if one takes the criteria that NHRIs

[90] Rules of Procedure of the Coordinating Committee of African National Institutions for the Promotion and Protection of Human Rights.

[91] Ibid, Art 9(b) and (c).

[92] Ibid, Art 18.

[93] Human Rights Watch, above n 49, at 71.

[94] International Council on Human Rights Policy, *Performance and Legitimacy: National Human Rights Institutions* (Geneva, ICHPR, 2000), 102.

have to meet to gain such status, some regulation over their work and accountability. While most of the criteria focus on the manner in which the institution was established (namely that it 'should be duly established by law, constitution or by decree'; 'shall be a national institution of a state party to the African Charter') there is reference to the requirement that the institution complies with the Paris Principles.[95] In addition, with the status comes certain 'rights and responsibilities' which include rights to be 'invited to sessions of the African Commission according to Rule 6 of the Rules and Procedures,' 'represented in public sessions of the Commission and its subsidiary bodies', to 'participate without voting rights in deliberations on issues which are of interest to them and to submit proposals which may be put to the vote at the request of any member of the Commission.'

In return for these rights, NHRIs have the duty to submit a report to the Commission every two years 'on its activities in the promotion and protection of the rights enshrined in the Charter.'[96] This is a very weak accountability mechanism, however. Although the African Commission has, on an ad hoc basis, produced lists of compliance with this requirement, there is no procedure for considering the content of the report, no institution has been called to account for its activities, and the reports have never been distributed at African Commission sessions or among other partners of the African Commission.[97]

In terms of how seriously the African Commission takes the criteria for affiliated status, although all applications are discussed in public sessions, it is little more than a bureaucratic exercise, checking that the relevant paperwork is provided, rather than any serious attempt to check the independence, credibility or effectiveness of the institution. Indeed, the African Commission seems uncomfortable adopting this regulatory role. This is even where the NHRI itself is requesting the African Commission to assist it by reviewing its compliance with the Paris Principles. For example, at the 28th session of the African Commission, the Niger Commission made a statement noting some difficulties with government interference with the independence of the Niger Commission (government officials to be members of the Commission). It was requesting affiliated status from the African Commission but asked that it review all those institutions with such status to ensure their compliance with the Paris Principles and request the government to withdraw the Bill undermining the independence of the Niger Commission. The African Commissioners stressed their support for the NHRI but said that the issue would be examined *in camera*. The Niger Commission was asked to apply formally to the African Commission for affiliated status, but

[95] African Commission on Human and Peoples' Rights, Resolution on the Granting of Observer Status to National Human Rights Institutions in Africa (1998), ACHPR /Res.31(XXIV)98, para 4(a).

[96] Ibid.

[97] Similar difficulties arise with respect to the obligations on NGOs to submit reports to international bodies. See JD Aston, 'The United Nations Committee on Non-Governmental Organizations: Guarding the Entrance to a Politically Divided House' (2001) 12(5) *EJIL* 943–62, at 961.

the chair of the African Commission urged all states not to interfere in the independence of national institutions. The Niger Commission was granted affiliated status at this same session. Rule 111 was mentioned and the need for urgent action, although it is not clear whether this was actually done. Although one Commissioner suggested that a resolution be adopted by the African Commission outlining how to deal with institutions which no longer complied with the criteria, no resolution was ever produced. Despite the chair of the African Commission stating that if the conditions under which the NHRI had been granted affiliated status ceased to exist the body would be de-affiliated, and that institutions should submit their new constitution or details to the ICC and African Commission, this was not followed through and there have been no instances of affiliated institutions being denied their status.

Again, in the consideration of the applications, the African Commission has focused on a simple compliance with the Paris Principles checklist, a bureaucratic exercise which looks at submission of relevant paperwork, rather than any meaningful engagement in how it operates in practice. At the 29th session when considering the application for affiliated status from the National Commission on Human Rights of Chad,[98] the rapporteur member of the African Commission noted the date of the application, the inclusion of the constitution, an overview of the institution's powers, its composition and various reports made by it. Having visited Chad and this Commission in his promotional capacity the member of the African Commission said he could therefore 'verify that it does indeed function.' Status was granted without debate.

Despite what one might imagine, the African Commission has also been willing to grant affiliated status to NHRIs which have not acquired ICC accreditation. Indeed, it is not apparent from discussions during the sessions whether the African Commission is indeed aware of which institution has accreditation and which does not. The procedure is dependent on the Commissioner as rapporteur checking the relevant documentation and probing into the institution in question, which rarely happens, or the Commissioner from the particular state giving a viewpoint on status. The latter has never occurred in public forum.

While having members of NHRIs sitting as African Commissioners may cause problems of conflict of interest, it does have the advantage of alerting the African Commission to debates before the ICC on the independence of that institution. For example, the application of the Nigerian Human Rights Commission was postponed for several sessions on the basis of continued concerns of its independence as there were representatives of government on its membership.[99]

[98] Chad has A(R) status before the ICC.

[99] Eg at the 27th session this was: National Human Rights Commission of Rwanda; Malawi Human Rights Commission and the National Human Rights Observatory of Algeria. At the 28th session: Senegalese Committee of Human Rights; the National Commission of Human Rights and Fundamental Freedoms of Niger and the National Commission for Democracy and Human Rights of Sierra Leone. At the 29th session: National Commission on Human Rights in Chad.

Overall, the African Commission has operated less as a forum by which affiliated status grants any formal indication of their legitimacy or independence, but sees them as an additional partner and affiliated status offering simply a formal manner in which to participate with them. On the one hand this rather pragmatic response may not cause difficulties. If NHRIs are simply another actor (state or non-state) on the international field, the African Commission may be interested in hearing their views. On the other, acquiring affiliated status may accord the NHRI some legitimacy at the domestic level, a status which it may not deserve. In addition, the space then accorded to an NHRI which is just another mouthpiece for government potentially restricts the space accorded to other actors, including NGOs, in the Commission's deliberations.

RE-ACCREDITATION AND REVIEW PROCESS

Once an NHRI has acquired accreditation by the ICC, or affiliated status by the African Commission, there has been very little further consideration of its status, despite changes in circumstance that may affect the independence of the institution or its compliance with the Paris Principles. Just as has been said of the NGO consultative status with ECOSOC, once the organisation is accredited,

> the review process is more like an automatic renewal process than an actual examination of the original requirements for accreditation. . . . The UN is not able to monitor NGOs' democracy, accountability and transparency, so the systems for ensuring them will have to come elsewhere or the UN will have to secure funding to undertake serious review processes.[100]

At present the ICC Rules of Procedure provide in Article 3(g):

> Where the circumstances of any member of the group of National Institutions change in any way which may affect its compliance with the Paris Principles, that member shall notify the Chairperson of those changes and the Chairperson shall place the matter before the accreditation sub-committee for review of that member's membership.
>
> Where in the opinion of the Chairperson of the ICC or of any member of the accreditation sub-committee, it appears that the circumstances of any member of the group of National Institutions may have changed in any way which affects its compliance with the Paris Principles, the Chairperson or Sub-Committee may initiate a review of that member's membership.
>
> On any such review the Chairperson or Sub-Committee shall have all the powers and responsibilities as in application under Rule 3.

With increased attention on the accreditation process of the ICC, as a means by which NHRIs can then participate in the UN Charter, and to a certain extent treaty body mechanisms, so there has been further attention to review and re-accreditation. As the Secretary-General of the UN has pointed out, if

[100] Lehr-Lehnardt, above n 5, at 36.

the accreditation procedures are to determine participation in its various forums, then there will need to be some re-evaluation of the NHRIs that are accredited to make sure they still comply with the Paris Principles. This could be done by inserting such a clause in the ICC Rules of Procedure for it to happen every five years.[101] As a result of this recommendation, the NI Unit, as Secretariat to the ICC, has started to consider how the re-accreditation and review process can be made more rigorous and has proposed that there be regular reassessment of accreditation.[102] Thus, if attention is to be focused on ICC accreditation as a means by which NHRIs can participate in the new Human Rights Council, then the NI Unit has suggested that: 'the existing national institutions already accredited by ICC go through a process of reassessment. The secretariat to ICC has committed to assisting in such a process and has already begun structuring information so that when ICC determines how it wishes to proceed, the review process can commence.'[103] It has drafted a timetable for review of NHRIs within the next five years.

With respect to changes in circumstances affecting compliance with the Paris Principles, the ICC has recommended that this could include the following:

—Fundamental limitations to the working climate of the NHRI as reflected by a national repressive regime and/or state coups.
—Adoption of a new legal framework, amendment of existing legal framework of NHRI or legal challenges to elements thereof.
—Discrepancies between the legal framework and the actual implementation, including in relation to appointment procedures of NHRI members.
—Repeated or gross biased statements by NHRIs in favour of particular interests or against specific groups which violate the values contained in the UN Paris Principles.[104]

A number of these issues, however, are not within the control of the NHRI itself, but subject to government or external influences. Yet, it is the NHRI which stands to lose its accreditation and any legitimacy gained in such a status. The NHRI is potentially being held responsible for activities which are beyond its control. For example, at the 17th session of the ICC in April 2006, it was noted that several NHRIs were being considered under the Early Warning Mechanism, a procedure designed to 'protect' NHRIs, but which the ICC said may have an impact on their accreditation. For example, there were 'reports on

[101] Enhancing the Participation of National Human Rights Institutions in the Work of the Commission on Human Rights and its Subsidiary Bodies, above n 89, at para 16.

[102] Process currently utilised by the International Coordinating Committee to Accredit National Human Rights Institutions in compliance with the Paris Principles and ensure that the Process is Strengthened with Appropriate Periodic Review and on Ways and Means of Enhancing Participation of National Human Rights Institutions in the work of the Commission, Report of the Secretary General, 25 January 2006, E/CN.4/2006/102, at para 22.

[103] Ibid, at para 22.

[104] ICC, Draft Proposal for ICC Re-Accreditation Procedures for NHRIs, 17th Session of the International Coordinating Committee of NHRIs, 10–11 April 2006, on file with author, para 2.2.

external pressure on the work' of the Kenyan National Human Rights Commission, lack of appointments to the National Human Rights Commission of Madagascar, and an 'alleged discrepancy between legal framework and appointment procedures applied for members of the Commission Natoinale des Droits de l'Homme et des Libertés Fondamentales' of Niger.[105] Where the political climate had created 'fundamental limitations' to the work of the National Human Rights Commission of Nepal, members of the ICC commented that this would be one issue to consider in terms of review and re-accreditation of an NHRI.

Although NHRIs are required to submit reports every two years to the African Commission, it is not clear what happens to these reports. There are no known instances of these being discussed or raised in public sessions and NHRIs themselves are not aware of whether they are discussed or deliberated upon by the Commission. It is also clear that not all NHRIs submit these reports, or submit them on time, and there has been little response from the Commission regarding their failure to do so.

There is a sense, however, among some NHRIs, that the African Commission should be stronger in ensuring compliance with the Paris Principles and removing affiliated status from those that do not comply.[106]

CONCLUSION

There are a number of benefits to having accountability considered at the international or regional levels. It lifts the issues out of domestic politics and potentially offers a more neutral environment in which to consider the activities of the NHRI. What is also clear, however, is how an NHRI is viewed at the international and regional levels has an impact on its legitimacy domestically.

However, so far, the UN and African bodies have advocated the establishment of some procedures to accredit NHRIs and their compliance with the Paris Principles, but have done little to actually analyse in detail how effective the institution is or make any public statement on those who fail to approach these basic standards.[107] All international and regional level bodies have encouraged states to establish NHRIs where none exist, without any serious consideration as to whether these might be the most appropriate mechanism to promote and protect human rights within that particular jurisdiction.[108]

One of the problems is that the international and regional bodies are attempting to fulfil a number of roles with respect to NHRIs. Some of them are trying to be both representative bodies which reflect the interests of their members, some of them are trying to act as a bridge between international institutions and

[105] Draft Report on ICC Activities, 2005–2006, April 2006, on file with author.
[106] Interview with member of NHRI, 7 April 2006.
[107] Human Rights Watch, above n 49, at 75.
[108] Ibid, at 76.

NHRIs, while they are also attempting to provide an avenue through which NHRIs can develop best practice. In addition, both the ICC, the African Commission on Human and Peoples' Rights, and to a much lesser degree, the African CCANI, are trying to perform a regulatory function. As the Rules of Procedure of the ICC note, its role is 'a representative body of NHRI established for the purpose of creating and strengthening NHRI which are in conformity with the Paris Principles. . . . It works to create and strengthen National Institutions and to ensure they conform to the Paris Principles.'[109] These do not sit well together and if the international and regional organisations are to take the role of NHRIs seriously, to prevent them being granted legitimacy without merit, then a serious consideration of what their role is and how they should be accrediting and assessing these institutions is needed.

[109] Rules of Procedure of the ICC, preamble.

7

Conclusion

NHRIs ARE NEW actors on the international and regional planes. While the UN, the African Commission and international law generally operate on the basis of a clear dichotomy between state and non-state actors, National Human Rights Institutions (NHRIs) challenge this separation. Requiring at the very least the commitment by the state to establish them in some official status, leaving aside whether the state then funds them or appoints their members, NHRIs are elevated into a position beyond an NGO. Yet, their effectiveness and their very nature requires them to operate separately from government and not be subject to its influence or control and therefore not to be viewed simply as part of the state machinery. At the national level, NHRIs have found it difficult to mediate this space, between the government on the one hand, and civil society on the other, especially when their ability to influence human rights promotion and protection in that society requires that they co-operate and work closely with both. This is complicated further by the knowledge that many NHRIs are closely connected to government and do not operate at a distance from them.

What is needed is a more nuanced and honest approach to the concept of independence. This needs to go beyond looking simply at the amount of funding, manner of appointment and composition of an NHRI, for example, to the nature of its relationship with government. In this respect it would be particularly useful, rather than seeing all NHRIs as the same, to distinguish between different institutions. For example, those established by constitution carry a certain weight compared with those established by decree. Any discussion of independence, accountability and accreditation needs to take this different status on board. In addition, it also needs to take account of the potential influence of other actors, whether they be civil society, parliamentarians or other stakeholders, on the NHRI.

This lack of a clear space at the national level has been played out at the international level, where the dichotomy of state/non-state is even more stark. Unlike NGOs, which fit more easily into the mould of a non-state actor, NHRIs can and are seen as both state and non-state actors. This has profound implications for how they participate in the UN Charter and treaty body mechanisms, the African Union (AU) and the African Commission on Human and Peoples' Rights.

With the adoption of Resolution 60/251 establishing the UN Human Rights Council, discussions on a Unified Standing Treaty Body, the establishment of an African Court on Human and Peoples' Rights, and the celebrations of the 25th anniversary of the African Charter on Human and Peoples' Rights, now is a opportune moment to have a more sophisticated and honest debate about the role of NHRIs in these arena. This may have implications for other actors, but if these international and regional bodies are to allow for increased participation of a variety of actors in their work, there need to be clearer levels of accountability applied to all if the systems are to maintain any integrity.

This requires a more detailed consideration of the concept of independence, as advocated by the Paris Principles, and others. This may require an examination of the utility of the Paris Principles and the appropriateness of more detailed guidance on effective NHRIs. It requires an understanding of the very specific role played by NHRIs and where they fit within a state/non-state dichotomy. It also necessitates a more in-depth consideration of which actors are responsible for which activities, beyond simply attributing it to the state or the NHRI.

This in turn will help to inform whether and how NHRIs should participate in the UN Human Rights Council and its subsidiary organs, any treaty bodies or Unified Treaty Body, the AU, African Commission on Human and Peoples' Rights, and other organs, and how to ensure a consistency of approach between them.

Unfortunately, any discussions of these issues are presently being driven primarily by NHRIs themselves, in the International Coordinating Committee of National Human Rights Institutions (ICC) in particular, with little outside input from other parties which may have less of a vested interest in ensuring participation of these institutions at the UN and African levels and may be able to offer some real challenges to how best to deal with these institutions. It is therefore the ICC which has set up two working groups to examine the role of NHRIs in the new Human Rights Council and in the UN treaty bodies respectively.[1]

What is clear is that NHRIs are in a potentially vulnerable, but also opportune position. Having not yet established any consistent role or space for themselves in the UN or African bodies, they have little precedent on which to rely. On the other hand, the UN and African bodies are looking to them to define their own role and regulate themselves. While NHRIs are going to have to tread carefully, equally it is important that other actors, whether they are NGOs, governments, UN and African bodies themselves, start to take more of an interest and role in these developments.

From the foregoing, a number of conclusions can be drawn. The ICC needs to be more forthright in how it advocates for more visible and formal status for NHRIs at the UN. It is the ICC who should take the lead on further discussion of the role of NHRIs at the international level, on the different types of NHRI

[1] At its 17th meeting in April 2006.

and on the concept of independence. This may help to assuage concerns among some NHRIs that the agenda of the ICC is being driven more by the National Institutions Unit of the OHCHR than by NHRIs themselves.

Similarly, at the regional level, NHRIs need to take greater responsibility for developing their own status, whether that be at the level of the African Union, sub-regionally, or before the African Charter on Human and Peoples' Rights organs. There have been enough initiatives, such as the AU conferences on NHRIs, recognition by sub-regional bodies in their formal documentation, the possibility of applying for affiliated status before the African Commission on Human and Peoples' Rights and recognition of the potential role of NHRIs in a merged Court that give a clear indication these regional bodies are open to NHRIs and embrace their participation. Yet NHRIs have so far not made full use of these opportunities available to them. It is in the hands of NHRIs to determine their own future.

More broadly, in order for the system to ensure accountability for the variety of actors that it now permits to participate, there needs to be an open, transparent and inclusive dialogue on responsibilities of each. Whether this is accomplished through legally binding rules (in the case of states) or more voluntary codes of conduct (in the case of others),[2] may be less important than actually ensuring a consistent and coherent approach to regulating the pluralist nature of the international and regional arenas.

[2] C Scott, 'Analysing Regulatory Space: Fragmented Resources and Institutional Design' [2001] *Public Law* 329–53, at 343.

Appendix I

THE PARIS PRINCIPLES

Principles Relating to the Status and Functioning of National Institutions for Protection and Promotion of Human Rights

Commission on Human Rights, March 1992 (resolution 1992/54); General Assembly Resolution A/RES/48/134 of 20 December 1993.

Competence and Responsibilities

1. A national institution shall be vested with competence to promote and protect human rights.

2. A national institution shall be given as broad a mandate as possible, which shall be clearly set forth in a constitutional or legislative text, specifying its composition and its sphere of competence.

3. A national institution shall, inter alia, have the following responsibilities:

(a) To submit to the Government, Parliament and any other competent body, on an advisory basis either at the request of the authorities concerned or through the exercise of its power to hear a matter without higher referral, opinions, recommendations, proposals and reports on any matters concerning the promotion and protection of human rights; the national institution may decide to publicize them; these opinions, recommendations, proposals and reports, as well as any prerogative of the national institution, shall relate to the following areas:

(i) Any legislative or administrative provisions, as well as provisions relating to judicial organizations, intended to preserve and extend the protection of human rights; in that connection, the national institution shall examine the legislation and administrative provisions in force, as well as bills and proposals, and shall make such recommendations as it deems appropriate in order to ensure that these provisions conform to the fundamental principles of human rights; it shall, if necessary, recommend the adoption of new legislation, the amendment of legislation in force and the adoption or amendment of administrative measures;

(ii) Any situation of violation of human rights which it decides to take up;
(iii) The preparation of reports on the national situation with regard to human rights in general, and on more specific matters;
(iv) Drawing the attention of the Government to situations in any part of the country where human rights are violated and making proposals to it for initiatives to put an end to such situations and, where necessary, expressing an opinion on the positions and reactions of the Government;

(b) To promote and ensure the harmonization of national legislation regulations and practices with the international human rights instruments to which the State is a party, and their effective implementation;

(c) To encourage ratification of the above-mentioned instruments or accession to those instruments, and to ensure their implementation;

(d) To contribute to the reports which States are required to submit to United Nations bodies and committees, and to regional institutions, pursuant to their treaty obligations and, where necessary, to express an opinion on the subject, with due respect for their independence;

(e) To cooperate with the United Nations and any other organization in the United Nations system, the regional institutions and the national institutions of other countries that are competent in the areas of the promotion and protection of human rights;

(f) To assist in the formulation of programmes for the teaching of, and research into, human rights and to take part in their execution in schools, universities and professional circles;

(g) To publicize human rights and efforts to combat all forms of discrimination, in particular racial discrimination, by increasing public awareness, especially through information and education and by making use of all press organs.

Composition and Guarantees of Independence and Pluralism

1. The composition of the national institution and the appointment of its members, whether by means of an election or otherwise, shall be established in accordance with a procedure which affords all necessary guarantees to ensure the pluralist representation of the social forces (of civilian society) involved in the promotion and protection of human rights, particularly by powers which will enable effective cooperation to be established with, or through the presence of, representatives of:

(a) Non-governmental organizations responsible for human rights and efforts to combat racial discrimination, trade unions, concerned social and professional organizations, for example, associations of lawyers, doctors, journalists and eminent scientists;

(b) Trends in philosophical or religious thought;

(c) Universities and qualified experts;

(d) Parliament;

(e) Government departments (if these are included, their representatives should participate in the deliberations only in an advisory capacity).

2. The national institution shall have an infrastructure which is suited to the smooth conduct of its activities, in particular adequate funding. The purpose of this funding should be to enable it to have its own staff and premises, in order to be independent of the Government and not be subject to financial control which might affect its independence.

3. In order to ensure a stable mandate for the members of the national institution, without which there can be no real independence, their appointment shall be effected by an official act which shall establish the specific duration of the mandate. This mandate may be renewable, provided that the pluralism of the institution's membership is ensured.

Methods of Operation

Within the framework of its operation, the national institution shall:

(a) Freely consider any questions falling within its competence, whether they are submitted by the Government or taken up by it without referral to a higher authority, on the proposal of its members or of any petitioner;

(b) Hear any person and obtain any information and any documents necessary for assessing situations falling within its competence;

(c) Address public opinion directly or through any press organ, particularly in order to publicize its opinions and recommendations;

(d) Meet on a regular basis and whenever necessary in the presence of all its members after they have been duly convened;

(e) Establish working groups from among its members as necessary, and set up local or regional sections to assist it in discharging its functions;

(f) Maintain consultation with the other bodies, whether jurisdictional or otherwise, responsible for the promotion and protection of human rights (in particular ombudsmen, mediators and similar institutions);

(g) In view of the fundamental role played by the non-governmental organizations in expanding the work of the national institutions, develop relations with the non-governmental organizations devoted to promoting and protecting human rights, to economic and social development, to combating racism, to protecting particularly vulnerable groups (especially children, migrant workers, refugees, physically and mentally disabled persons) or to specialized areas.

Additional Principles concerning the Status of Commissions with Quasi-jurisdictional Competence

A national institution may be authorized to hear and consider complaints and petitions concerning individual situations. Cases may be brought before it by individuals, their representatives, third parties, non-governmental organizations, associations of trade unions or any other representative organizations. In such circumstances, and without prejudice to the principles stated above concerning the other powers of the commissions, the functions entrusted to them may be based on the following principles:

(a) Seeking an amicable settlement through conciliation or, within the limits prescribed by the law, through binding decisions or, where necessary, on the basis of confidentiality;

(b) Informing the party who filed the petition of his rights, in particular the remedies available to him, and promoting his access to them;

(c) Hearing any complaints or petitions or transmitting them to any other competent authority within the limits prescribed by the law;

(d) Making recommendations to the competent authorities, especially by proposing amendments or reforms of the laws, regulations and administrative practices, especially if they have created the difficulties encountered by the persons filing the petitions in order to assert their rights.

Appendix II

AFRICAN COMMISSION ON HUMAN AND PEOPLES' RIGHTS

RESOLUTION ON THE GRANTING OF OBSERVER STATUS TO NATIONAL HUMAN RIGHTS INSTITUTIONS IN AFRICA

ACHPR/RES.31 (XXIV) 98

Background

In the preamble of the African Charter on Human and Peoples' Rights adopted at the 18th Conference of Heads of State and Government in Nairobi in June 1981, Member States of the Organization of African Unity reaffirmed,

> their adherence to the principles of human and peoples' rights and freedoms contained in the declarations, conventions and other instruments adopted by the Organization of African Unity, the Movement of Non-Aligned Countries and United Nations.

In the same preamble, African Countries pledged to '. . . coordinate and intensify their cooperation and efforts to achieve a better life for the peoples of Africa and to promote international cooperation having due regard to the Charter of the United Nations and the Universal Declaration of Human Rights.'

With the aim of concretising this commitment, Article 26 of the African Charter on Human and Peoples' Rights stipulates that:

> States Parties to the present Charter shall have the duty to guarantee the independence of the Courts and shall allow the establishment and improvement of appropriate national institutions entrusted with the promotion and protection of the rights and freedoms guaranteed by the present Charter.

The use of the word 'allow' suggests not just encouraging and promoting the establishment of National Institutions, but developing a mutually co-operative relationship in order to 'promote and ensure, through teaching, education and publication, respect for the rights and freedoms contained in the present charter . . . ' (Article 25).

National Institutions, therefore, are an essential partner in the implementation of the Charter at National Level. It is noted that the Mauritius Plan of Action (1996–2001) envisaged workshops on national institutions as one of its promotional activities. It also seeks the co-operation of national institutions in fulfilling its mandate of promoting and protecting human and peoples' rights.

Finally, the Second Seminar of Ambassadors of African States to the OAU held in Addis Ababa, 8–9 September 1998 recognised the importance of National Institutions and urged governments to accord them appropriate support.

African States in general and the African Commission on Human and Peoples' Rights in particular took an active part in the deliberations of the World Conference on Human Rights which was held in Vienna in June 1993. The Vienna Conference's Declaration and Programme of Action reaffirmed:

> the important and constructive role played by national institutions for the promotion and protection of Human Rights, in particular in their advisory role to the competent authorities, their role at remedying human rights violations, in the dissemination of information and education in human rights.

The World Conference on Human Rights also encouraged 'the establishment and strengthening of national institutions . . .' and recognised '. . . that it is the right of each State to choose the framework which is best suited to its particular needs at the national level . . .'

At this conference a formal status was granted to the International Committee for Coordination of National Institutions as a statutory liaison instrument of the United Nations system. This Committee shall organise a biennial world meeting of national institutions.

At the international level, the United Nations Human Rights Commission approved by its Resolution 1992/54 of the 3 March 1992 under the heading 'Principles Relating to the Status of National Institutions,' also known as the 'Paris Principles' rules which define the mandate of such institutions. The General Assembly of the United Nations endorsed these principles in its Resolution 48/144 of 20 December 1993.

The objective of these principles is to guarantee the independence of national institutions in their work and pluralism in their composition. The central mission of the national institutions is to play an advisory role to the government, parliament and other relevant bodies and authorities involved in giving opinion and making recommendations on all issues related to the promotion and protection of human rights.

In Africa, the trend to establish national institutions has continued to develop especially after 1991. At present Africa has more than twenty national human rights institutions which are represented in the International Coordination Committee by Cameroon, Morocco, South Africa and Togo.

At the first conference of national human rights institutions in Africa held in Yaounde, Cameroon, from 5–7 February 1996, participants adopted the Yaounde Declaration which commended '. . . the creation of new National Institutions in Africa . . . ' and expressed the hope that these institutions will be given '. . . a proper representative status on the African Commission.' At the second conference of African National Institutions held in Durban, 1–3 July 1998, the need for a clear relationship and a unique status in the African Commission were reiterated.

Since the Mauritius session, the issue of African national human rights institutions has always been included on the agenda of meetings of the Commission. A paper on this subject was presented by Commissioner K Rezag-Bara at the 21st Ordinary Session of the Commission held in Nouakchott, Mauritania in April 1997. The Commission decided at its 22nd Session held in Banjul in November 1997 to entrust Commissioners K Rezag-Bara and Barney Pityana with the task of preparing a draft resolution on the advisory status of national institutions in the African Commission on Human and Peoples' Rights. The matter was deferred for finalisation at this session.

Therefore, the African Commission on Human and Peoples' Rights, meeting at its 24th Ordinary Session from 22–31 October 1998, in Banjul, The Gambia:

Considering the preamble of the African Charter on Human and Peoples' Rights which reaffirms the adherence of African States to 'human and peoples' rights and freedoms contained in the declarations, conventions and other instruments adopted by the organization of African Unity, the Movement of Non-Aligned countries and the United Nations';

Considering that Article 26 of the African Charter on Human and Peoples' Rights stipulates that 'States Parties to the present Charter shall have the duty to . . . allow the establishment and the improvement of appropriate national institutions entrusted with the promotion and protection of rights';

Considering the recommendation adopted in the Programme of Action of the World Conference on Human Rights held in Vienna, Austria in June 1993 and United Nations resolutions on human rights, particularly resolution 1992/54 of 3 March 1992 of the Commission Human Rights and resolution 48/134 of 20 December 1993 of the United Nations General Assembly;

Considering the decisions, resolutions, recommendations and the final declaration adopted by the first conference of national human rights institutions in Africa held in Yaounde, Cameroon from 5–7 February 1996 and the second conference held in Durban, South Africa from 1–3 July 1998;

Convinced of the importance of the role of national institutions in the promotion and protection of human rights and in creating public awareness in Africa with regard to the institutional defence of human rights;

1. COMMENDS the increasing interests shown by African states in establishing and strengthening national institutions for the protection and promotion of human rights based on the principles of independence and pluralism.

2. RECOGNIZES that it is the right of each state to establish, according to its sovereign prerogatives and within the most appropriate legislative framework, a national institution charged with the promotion and protection of human rights according to internationally recognized norms.

3. NOTES WITH SATISFACTION the significant participation of African National Institutions in the deliberations of the sessions of the African Commission on Human and Peoples' Rights and registers positively the wish

expressed by several institutions to be granted an observer status with the Commission.

4. DECIDES to grant special observer status to any African national institution established in Africa and functioning according to internationally recognized norms and standards.

(a) that the following criteria for the status of affiliated institution shall apply:

- the national institution should be duly established by law, constitution or by decree;
- that it shall be a national institution of a state party to the African Charter;
- that the national institution should conform to the Principles relating to the Status of National Institutions, also known as the Paris Principles, adopted by the General Assembly of the United Nations under Resolution 48/144 of 20th December 1993.
- that a National Institution shall formally apply for status in the African Commission;

(b) that such institutions shall have the following rights and responsibilities.

- be invited to sessions of the African Commission according to rule 6 of the Rules and Procedures,
- be represented in public sessions of the commission and its subsidiary bodies,
- participate, without voting rights, in deliberations on issues which are of interest to them and to submit proposals which may be put to the vote at the request of any member of the Commission;

(c) that any national institution shall be required to submit reports to the Commission every two years on its activities in the promotion and protection of the rights enshrined in the Charter and;

(d) that the National Institution will assist the Commission in the promotion and protection of human rights at national level.

Banjul, 31 October 1998

Appendix III

THE INTERNATIONAL COORDINATING COMMITTEE OF NATIONAL INSTITUTIONS FOR THE PROMOTION AND PROTECTION OF HUMAN RIGHTS

RULES OF PROCEDURE

Preamble

The International Coordinating Committee is a representative body of National Human Rights Institutions established for the purpose of creating and strengthening National Human Rights Institutions which are in conformity with the Paris Principles.[1] It performs this role through encouraging international co-ordination of joint activities and co-operation among these National Human Rights Institutions, organising International Conferences, liaison with the United Nations and other international organisations and, where requested, assisting governments to establish a National Institution. It works to create and strengthen National Institutions and to ensure they conform to the Paris Principles.

1. Name

The name of the committee is the International Co-ordinating Committee of National Human Rights Institutions for the Promotion and Protection of Human Rights (the ICC).

2. Functions

The functions of the ICC are:

(a) To co-ordinate, at an international level, the activities of National Human Rights Institutions established in conformity with the Principles Relating to the Status and Functioning of National Institutions for the Promotion and Protection of Human Rights (the Paris Principles).

[1] Commission on Human Rights Resolution 1992/54 of 3 March 1992, annex *(Official Records of the Economic and Social Council, 1992, Supplement No 2* (E/1992/22), ch II, sect. A); General Assembly resolution 48/134 of 20 December1993, annex.

(b) To support the creation and strengthening of National Human Rights Institutions (National Institutions) in conformity with the Paris Principles.

(c) To ensure regular contacts with the Office of the United Nations High Commissioner for Human Rights and the other international organisations concerned with the promotion and protection of human rights.

(d) To plan and organise with the host institution International Conferences for National Institutions in co-operation with the Office of the United Nations High Commissioner for Human Rights.

(e) To encourage and assist as requested the organisation of Regional Workshops of National Institutions.

(f) To encourage co-operation amongst National Institutions.

(g) To follow up on and, where appropriate, implement recommendations of International Conferences of National Institutions and other relevant United Nations resolutions.

(h) To liaise with such other organisations as may be engaged in the promotion and protection of human rights.

(i) To undertake such other functions as are referred to it by International Conferences of National Institutions and consider matters referred to it by regional meetings.

3. Membership of the Group of National Institutions

(a) Only National Institutions which comply with the Paris Principles shall be eligible to be members of the group of National Institutions.

(b) Only one National Institution per state shall be eligible to be a voting member. Where more than one institution in a state qualifies for membership the state shall have one speaking right, one voting right, and if elected one committee member. The choice of an institution to represent the National Institutions of a particular state shall be for the relevant institutions to determine.

(c) Any National Institution seeking membership shall apply to the Chairperson of the ICC. That National Institution shall supply, in support of its application:

- a copy of the legislation or other instrument by which it is established and empowered
- an outline of its organisational structure including staff complement and annual budget
- a copy of its most recent annual report or equivalent document

- a detailed statement showing that it complies with the Paris Principles or, alternatively, an outline of any respects in which it does not so comply and any proposals to ensure compliance.

(d) All questions of membership, including whether a National Institution complies with the Paris Principles, shall be decided by the ICC or any membership sub-committee it may establish. No decision adverse to the application for membership of a National Institution shall be made without consultation with that institution.

(e) Should the application for membership of any National Institution be declined by reason of its failure to comply with the Paris Principles, the ICC or its delegate may consult further with that institution concerning compliance.

(f) Any National Institution whose application for membership is declined may, with the consent of the ICC, attend meetings or workshops of the group as observer and may reapply for membership at any time.

(g) Where the circumstances of any member of the group of National Institutions change in any way which may affect its compliance with the Paris Principles, that member shall notify the Chairperson of those changes and the Chairperson shall place the matter before the accreditation sub-committee for review of that member's membership. Where, in the opinion of the Chairperson of the ICC or of any member of the accreditation sub-committee, it appears that the circumstances of any member of the group of National Institutions may have changed in any way which affects its compliance with the Paris Principles, the Chairperson or sub-committee may initiate a review of that member's membership. On any such review the Chair or sub-committee shall have all the powers and responsibilities as in an application under Rule 3.

4. Regional Groupings of Members

For the purpose of ensuring a fair balance of regional representation on the ICC the following regional groups are established:

- Africa
- Europe
- the Americas
- Asia-Pacific

(b) The members within any regional group may establish such subregional groupings as they wish.

(c) The members of regional groups may establish their own procedures concerning meetings and activities.

(d) Regional groups are to elect four members to represent them on the ICC on a regional or a sub-regional basis as they choose.

5. Membership of the ICC

(a) Membership is the prerogative of a National Institution not of any individual and is restricted to institutions approved to be members pursuant to clause 3 of these Rules. There shall be 16 members of the ICC comprising four representatives from each of the regional groups.

(b) Regional group representatives are eligible for re-election.

(c) Regional group representatives on the ICC shall be elected from within each regional group for a term of two years.

6. Chairperson and Deputy-Chairperson of the International Coordinating Committee

(a) At its first meeting following adoption of these rules the members of the ICC present shall elect one of their number to be the Chairperson and another to be the Deputy Chairperson.

(b) The roles of Chairperson and Deputy Chairperson attach to the National Institution whose representative is elected.

(c) The Chairperson and Deputy-Chairperson shall serve for a term of one year and may be re-elected at the conclusion of the term.

7. Liaison with Other Human Rights Institutions and NGOs

(a) The ICC may liaise with other human rights institutions including the International Ombudsman Institute and non-governmental organisations.

(b) The ICC may decide to grant such organisations observer status at any meetings or workshops of the group of National Institutions.

8. Meetings

(a) A meeting of the ICC shall be held in conjunction with the annual meeting of the Commission for Human Rights.

(b) A meeting of the ICC shall be held in conjunction with the bi-annual International Conference on National Institutions. Otherwise, the ICC shall meet at such times and places as it shall decide.

9. Conduct of Business

(a) English/French/Spanish shall be the working languages of the ICC.

(b) A majority of the Members of the ICC shall constitute a quorum.

(c) An agenda for each meeting shall be drawn up by the Chairperson in consultation with the Members. Agenda items may be added at the meeting if approved by a majority of the Members present.

(d) Members of the ICC shall be represented by duly authorized representatives of the institutional members concerned who may be accompanied at meetings by such advisers from the institution as they may require.

(e) Each member shall have one vote. Where possible decisions of the ICC shall be reached by consensus. When consensus is not possible, decisions shall be by a majority of members present and voting. In the event of an equality of votes, the proposal being voted on shall be regarded as being defeated.

(f) Representatives of National Institutions established in accordance with the Paris Principles, other than ICC members, are welcome to attend meetings.

(g) The Chairperson, after consultation with ICC members, may invite National Institutions who are not members of the ICC and any other person or institution to participate in the work of the ICC as an observer without the right to vote.

10. Further Procedure

Should any question concerning the procedure of the ICC arise which is not provided for by these rules the ICC may adopt such procedure as it thinks fit.

11. Amendment of Rules of Procedure

These Rules of Procedure may be amended only by an International Conference of National Human Rights Institutions.

Adopted 15 April 2000
And as amended 13 April 2002

Appendix IV

RULES OF PROCEDURE OF THE INTERNATIONAL COORDINATING COMMITTEE SUB-COMMITTEE ON ACCREDITATION*

1. Mandate

In accordance with the Rules of Procedure of the International Coordination Committee of National Institutions for the Promotion and Protection of Human Rights (ICC), the Sub- Committee on Accreditation has the mandate to review and analyse accreditation applications forwarded by the ICC Chairperson and to make recommendations to ICC members on the compliance of applicants with the Paris Principles.

2. Composition of the Sub-Committee

2.1. For the purpose of ensuring a fair balance of regional representation on the Sub-Committee on Accreditation, it shall be composed of one (1) ICC accredited national institution for each of the four (4) regional groupings as established by the ICC Rules of Procedure, namely Africa, Americas, Asia-Pacific, and Europe.

2.2. Members are appointed by Regional Groupings for a term of two (2) years renewable.

2.3. The Sub-Committee on Accreditation designates by consensus, for a term of two years renewable, one of its members to act as Chair of the Sub-Committee.

2.4 The Office of the United Nations High Commissioner for Human Rights shall be a permanent observer to the Committee and in its capacity as Secretariat of the ICC, support the Committee's work, serve as a focal point on all communications and maintain records as appropriate on behalf of the ICC Chairperson.

* Adopted by the members of the International Coordinating Committee at its 15th session, held on 14 September 2004, Seoul, Republic of Korea.

3. Functions

3.1. Each Regional Grouping Representative to the Sub-Committee on Accreditation shall facilitate the application process for national institutions in the region.

3.2. The Regional Grouping Representative shall supply national institutions from their region with all relevant information pertaining to the accreditation process, including a description of the process, requirements and timelines.

3.3. In accordance with the ICC Rules of Procedure (art 3), any national institution seeking membership shall apply to the ICC Chairperson, supplying support documents through the ICC Secretariat.

3.4. These applications and support documents shall be provided to the ICC Chairperson no later than two (2) months prior to the meeting of the ICC.

3.5. Applications and documents submitted after this delay will only be examined during the following year's meeting of the ICC, unless the situation warrants otherwise, as determined by the ICC Chairperson.

3.6. The ICC Chairperson will ensure that copies of the applications and supporting documentation are provided to each member of the Sub-Committee on Accreditation.

3.7. The ICC Chairperson, with support from the Office of the United Nations High Commissioner for Human Rights, will also provide a summary of particular issues for consideration by the Sub-Committee.

4. Procedures

4.1. The Sub-Committee on Accreditation will meet before and during the annual meeting of the ICC in order to review new applications, review additional information submitted on applications presented previously, and prepare recommendations.

4.2. The meeting will be restricted to members of the Sub-Committee on Accreditation and the Office of the United Nations High Commissioner for Human Rights.

4.3 Additional meetings of the Committee may be convened by the Chair with the agreement of the ICC Chairperson and Accreditation Sub-Committee members.

5. Accreditation Classifications

In accordance with the Paris Principles and the ICC Rules of Procedures, the different classifications for accreditation used by the Committee are:

A: Compliance with the Paris Principles;
A(R): Accreditation with reserve–granted where preliminary analysis indicates compliance with the Principles but insufficient documentation is submitted to confer A status;
B: Observer Status-Not fully in compliance with the Paris Principles or insufficient information provided to make a determination;
C: Non-compliant with the Paris Principles.

6. Report and Recommendations

6.1 The Chair of the Sub-Committee on Accreditation will present a report with recommendations and rationale to members of the ICC for their decision.

6.2. The ICC Chairperson will indicate in the report of the meeting decisions taken by ICC members with regards to applications for accreditation.

6.3. The Chairperson of the ICC will inform applicant institutions of the decisions taken and their rationale by ICC members.

Appendix V

RULES OF PROCEDURE OF THE COORDINATING COMMITTEE OF AFRICAN NATIONAL INSTITUTIONS FOR THE PROMOTION AND PROTECTION OF HUMAN RIGHTS

1. Name and Attributions

Article 1

Within the African Group, a Committee known and called the Coordinating Committee of African National Institutions for the Promotion and Protection of Human Rights (hereinafter called 'the Committee') is established with the English acronym CCANI.

Article 2

The African Group is composed of all the African National Human Rights Institutions (NHRIs) accredited or not by the International Coordinating Committee of National Human Rights Institutions (ICC).

Article 3

All African NHRI shall be registered at the permanent Secretariat of the Committee.

Article 4

The functions of the Committee, include, *inter alia:*

- To facilitate the co-ordination of the activities of African NHRIs;
- To encourage the establishment of new NHRIS in the continent in conformity with the Paris Principles;
- To prepare and organise meetings of the Committee;
- To prepare the strategic and work plans and budget to be approved by the Committee;
- To encourage co-operation among African national institutions and with intergovernmental and non-governmental organisations;
- To ensure follow-up and implementation of recommendations of the regional meetings of African NHRIs, the ICC, United Nations bodies, and other institutions with which the Committee co-operates; and
- To undertake all other tasks as decided by the Conference.

2. Composition and Membership

Article 5

(a) The Committee is composed of eleven (11) NHRIs from among African countries representing the five geographic regions of the continent, namely: Central Africa, East Africa, North Africa, Southern Africa and West Africa.

(b) Representation is proportional to the number of NHRIs from each region provided that no region is represented by more than three members at any one time.

(c) The Conference can change the representation of the Committee.

(d) The Committee can also allow other national institutions, intergovernmental and governmental agencies and NGOs to take part in its activities as observers.

Article 6

(a) Members are elected to serve for a two-year period renewable once.

(b) Members serve not in their personal capacity but as representatives of their institutions and regions.

Article 7

(a) If in the majority opinion of the Committee, an institution does not comply with the Paris Principles or is not discharging its functions as a Member of the Committee, an *ad hoc* Committee shall be established to investigate the matter.

(b) The ad hoc committee shall within ninety days make a report to the Committee which shall recommend on whether to suspend the membership of the Member or take such other steps as it may deem necessary to assist the Member.

(c) A recommendation may be made to the ICC Credential's Committee to revisit the accreditation of the NHRI in question.

Article 8

Where a vacancy occurs in the ICC as a result of termination of membership, resignation, death or any other reason, the replacement shall come from the same region in which the vacancy occurred.

3. Elections

Article 9

(a) Members of the Committee are elected from a proposal made by sub-regional organs at the bi-annual conference of African NHRIs.

(b) Only African NHRIs duly accredited by the ICC can be elected to serve at the Committee.

(c) Only NHRIs duly accredited by the ICC shall have the right to vote.

(d) Elections shall be held by a show of hands or at the request of a Member through secret ballot.

Article 10

(a) Voting on substantive and procedural matters in the Committee, unless otherwise decided, is by a show of hands. Any Member may request a roll-call vote which shall be undertaken in alphabetical order of those Members present. In all roll-call votes each Member shall reply 'yes,' 'no' or 'abstention.' The vote of each Member shall be recorded in the minutes.

(b) During voting there shall be no interruption unless a Member raises a point of order relating to the matter on which the ballot is being held. The Chairperson may allow Members to intervene briefly, whether before the vote commences or when the vote is closed, but solely to explain abstention relating to the matter being voted upon.

(c) Decisions are reached by consensus. In cases where a consensus may not be reached, a decision will be taken by vote. Agreement will be reached by a simple majority of votes cast of the Members present and voting in accordance with the quorum under article 15.

(d) In the case of a tied vote, the Chairperson shall have a casting vote.

(e) Only one institution from any country can be a Member of the Committee with the right to vote.

4. Meeting Conduct

Article 11

During the debate of any matter a Member may, at any time, raise a point of order and the Chairperson shall immediately decide on the point of order. If a Member appeals the decision of the Chairperson, the appeal shall immediately be put to a vote. If the Chairperson's ruling is not over-ruled by a simple majority of the Members present, it shall be maintained.

Article 12

The Chairperson may limit the time accorded to each Member on any matter. When the time allotted for debate is limited and a speaker spends more time than allotted, the Chairperson may call that Member to order.

Article 13

(a) The Chairperson may, during a discussion, read out the list of speakers and with the approval of the Committee, declare the list closed. Where there are no more speakers, the Chairperson may, with the approval of the Committee declare the discussion closed.

(b) The Chairperson may also decide to close discussion on any matter if in the Chairperson's opinion the matter has been discussed enough and a decision can be reached.

Article 14

(a) A provisional agenda and all relevant documents relating to each item of each session of the Committee shall be distributed to the Members and other institutions at least three weeks prior to each session.

(b) At the beginning of each session, the Committee shall adopt an agenda.

(c) The Committee may revise the agenda during a session, adjourn, cancel or amend items.

Article 15

(a) The Committee shall meet at least once a year in ordinary session, and where necessary during meetings of the ICC, the United Nations Commission on Human Rights or meetings of the African Commission on Human and Peoples' Rights or elsewhere as decided.

(b) The Committee shall ensure that no Member or region hosts the Conference in two consecutive sessions.

(c) A quorum of the Committee consists of five (5) members present.

Article 16

(a) The working languages of the Committee shall be French and English.

(b) At the end of each session, the Committee may issue a press release to the media and public on its activities.

5. Steering Committee

Article 17

(a) A Steering Committee of the Committee shall be constituted comprising four (4) Members including:

- the present Chairperson as host of the Biannual Conference;
- the next biannual Conference host as First Vice-Chairperson;
- the last Conference host as Second Vice-Chairperson; and
- and the Chairperson of the Member hosting the Secretariat.

(b) The Chairperson is the spokesperson for African NHRIs at all levels and shall represent the Committee where the interests of African NHRIs require.

(c) The Chairperson may delegate to a Vice-Chairperson or any other Member of the Committee.

Article 18

All African NHRIs are required to provide their annual report(s) every two years to the Chairperson and the Secretariat.

6. Secretariat

Article 19

(a) The Secretariat shall implement the policies and decisions of the Committee.

(b) The Secretariat of the Committee is in South Africa for the first three years. The Committee shall decide at the end of that period, where to establish its permanent Secretariat.

Article 20

(a) The Secretariat will be headed by an Executive Director responsible for:

- Preparation of projects for the Committee;
- The drawing up, with the Chairperson of the Committee, the provisional agenda for each session;
- Facilitating the establishment of new NHRIs in conformity with the Paris Principles;
- Keeping records of the Committee meetings;
- Maintaining the archives of the Committee; and
- Performing any other task as may be assigned to her or him by the Committee.

(b) The Executive Director is appointed for a fixed term. Until such time as the Secretariat becomes its own legal person, the Executive Director shall be an employee of the host Member. The Executive Direction shall report to the Committee Chairperson on policy matters and to the Chairperson of the host Member on administrative issues.

(c) The Executive Director participates in all meetings of the Committee without a right to vote.

Article 21

(a) Projects prepared by the Secretariat including the budget shall be approved by the Steering Committee in consultation with the CCANI Members.

(b) Provision shall be made in the budget for the Chairperson and Vice-Chairperson to travel on Committee business.

(c) The Secretariat will source its funds from grants, donations or contributions from Members of the Committee.

7. Final Dispositions

Article 22

In case of dissolution, the Committee shall determine how to dispose of its resources.

Article 23

Cases not foreseen in the present Rules of Procedure shall be presented for amendment to the Conference of African National Human Rights Institutions through the Secretariat. Amendments may only be adopted by an affirmative vote of a 2/3 majority of those Members present.

Article 24

The present Rules of Procedure may only come into force after adoption by the Conference of African National Human Rights Institutions.

Adopted in Kampala, Uganda on 15 August 2002

Bibliography

Articles and Books

ADDO, M, *Human Rights Standards and the Responsibility of Transnational Corporations* (The Hague, Kluwer Law International, 1999).

ALSTON, P, *Non-State Actors and Human Rights* (Oxford, Oxford University Press, 2005).

ALSTON, AP, 'The "Not-a-Cat" Syndrome: Can the International Human Rights Regime Accommodate Non-State Actors?' in P Alston, *Non-State Actors and Human Rights* (Oxford, Oxford University Press, 2005).

Amnesty International, 'Cameroon fails to protect the Fundamental Human Rights of its Citizens,' AI Index: AFR 17/06/99, 9 November 1999.

ASTON, JD, 'The United Nations Committee on Non-Governmental Organizations: Guarding the Entrance to a Politically Divided House'(2001) 12(5) *EJIL* 943–62.

BALDWIN, R, and CAVE, M, *Understanding Regulation: Theory, Strategy and Practice* (Oxford, Oxford University Press, 1999).

BARNETT, MN, and FINNEMORE, M, 'The Politics, Power, and Pathologies of International Organizations' (1999) 53(4) *International Organization* 699–732.

BARTHOLOGMEUSZ, L, 'The *Amicus Curiae* before International Courts and Tribunals'(2005) 5 *Non-State Actors and International Law* 209–86.

BERLIN, D, 'The Key to Green Power–Explaining NGO Influence in Global Environmental Governance Structure' prepared for NISA-NOPSA Conference, Reykjavik, 11–13 August 2005, Workshop Globalization as Individualization and Destabilization.

BHADAIN, V, 'The Institution of the Ombudsman in Mauritius, in K Hossain et al, *Human Rights Commissions and Ombudsman Offices. National Experiences Throughout the World* (The Hague, Kluwer Law International, 2001) 315–29.

BIANCHI, A, 'Globalization of Human Rights: The Role of Non-State Actors', in G Teubner (ed), *Global Law without a State* (Dartmouth, Aldershot, 1996).

BIZJAK, I, 'The Role and Experience of an Ombudsman in a New Democracy'(1998) 2 *International Ombudsman Yearbook* 57–62.

BLACK, J, 'Regulatory Conversations' (2002) 29(1) *Journal of Law and Society* 163–96.

BODANSKY, D, 'The Legitimacy of International Governance: A Coming Challenge for International Environmental Law?'(1999) 93 *American Journal of International Law* 596–624.

BREEN, C, 'Rationalising the Work of UN Human Rights Bodies or Reducing the Input of NGOs? The Changing Role of Human Rights NGOs at the United Nations' (2005) 5 *Non-State Actors and International Law* 101–26.

BURDEKIN, B, 'Human Rights Commissions' in K Hossain, L Besselink, H Selaisse and E Volker (eds), *National Human Rights Commissions and Ombudsman Offices:*

National Experiences Throughout the World (Dordrecht, Kluwer Law International, 2001) 801–34.

CARDENAS, S, 'Emerging Global Actors: The United Nations and National Human Rights Institutions'(2003) 9 *Global Governance* 23–42.

CARVER, R, and HUNT, P, 'Human Rights Institutions in Africa' in K Hossain, L Besselink, H Selaisse and E Volker (eds), *National Human Rights Commissions and Ombudsman Offices: National Experiences Throughout the World* (Dordrecht, Kluwer Law International, 2000) 801.

CHANDLER, D, 'The Road to Military Humanitarianism: How the Human Rights NGOs Shaped a New Humanitarian Agenda'(2001) 23 *HRQ* 678–700.

CHARNOVITZ, 'Two Centres of Participation: NGOs and International Governance' (1997) 18 *Michigan Journal of International Law* 183.

CHENG, B, 'Introduction to Subjects of International Law' in M Bedjaoui (ed), *International Law: Achievements and Prospects* (Paris, UNESCO, 1991) 23.

CLAPHAM, A, *Human Rights in the Private Sphere* (Oxford, Oxford University Press, 1993).

—— 'Defining the Role of Non-Governmental Organizations with Regard to the UN Human Rights Treaty Bodies' in AF Bayefsky (ed), *The UN Human Rights Treaty System in the 21st Century* (Dordrecht, Kluwer Law International, 2000) 183–94.

Commonwealth Secretariat, *National Human Rights Institutions. Best Practice*, (London, Commonwealth Secretariat, 2001).

Commonwealth Workshop on National Human Rights Institutions, Ottowa, 30 September–2 October 1992.

CULLEN, H, and MORROW, K, 'International Civil Society in International Law: The Growth of NGO Participation'(2001) 1 *Non-State Actors and International Law* 7–39.

DAY, P, and KLEIN, R, *Accountabilities. Five Public Services* (London, Tavistock Publications, 1987).

DECAUX, E, 'Evolution and Perspectives for National Institutions in the Promotion and Protection of Human Rights: Their Contribution to the Prevention of Human Rights Violations'(2001) 67 *International Studies in Human Rights* 233–43.

DICKSON, B, 'Human Rights Commissions: A Unique Role to Play, Now and in the Future', 27 *Human Rights*, Summer 2000.

—— 'The Contribution of Human Rights Commissions to the Protection of Human Rights'[2003] *Public Law* 272–85.

—— Chief Commissioner, Northern Ireland Human Rights Commission, Address to the Workshop on the Paris Principles, Tirana, Albania, 5 May 2004, www.nihrc.org.

DORSEY, E, and PIGOTT, B, 'The UN System and NGOs: New Relationships for a New Era?' in UN, *The UN System and NGOs: New Relationships for a New Era?, 25th United Nations Issues Conference 1994* (Iowa, Stanley Foundation, 1994) 14–15.

EARLE, P, 'National Human Rights Institutions and the Human Rights Approach to Development', Background Paper for the Regional Workshop on the Role of National Human Rights Institutions and Other Mechanisms in Promoting and Protecting Economic, Social and Cultural Rights, Human Rights Council of Australia

EBRAHIM, H, *The Soul of a Nation: Constitution-Making in South Africa* (Oxford, Oxford University Press, 1999).

EDWARDS, M, HULME, D, and WALLACE, T, 'NGOs in a Global Future: Marrying Local Delivery to Worldwide Leverage'(1999) 19 *Public Administration and Development* 117–36.

EVANS, C, 'Human Rights Commissions and Religious Conflict in Asia-Pacific Region'(2004) 53 *ICLQ* 713–29.

FINNEMORE, M, 'International Organizations as Teachers of Norms: The United Nations Educational, Scientific and Cultural Organization and Science Policy' (1993) 47(4) *International Organization* 565–97.

FOMBAD, CM, 'Election Management Bodies in Africa: Cameroon's National Elections Observatory in Perspective' (2003) 3(1) *African Human Rights Law Journal* 25–51.

FRANCK, T, *The Power of Legitimacy Among Nations* (Oxford, Oxford University Press, 1990).

—— *Fairness in International Law and Institutions* (Oxford, Clarendon Press, 1995).

FREUDENSCHUSS-REICHL, I, 'Agreement Making and Implementation: An Analysis of International Negotiations'(2002) 2 *Non-State Actors and International Law* 119–39.

GALLAGHER, A, 'Making Human Rights Treaty Obligations a Reality: Working With New Actors and Partners' in P Alston and J Crawford, *The Future of UN Human Rights Treaty Monitoring* (Cambridge, Cambridge University Press, 2000).

GALLAROTTI, GM, 'The Limits of International Organization: Systematic Failure in the Management of International Relations'(1991) 45(2) *International Organization* 183–220.

GLASER, D, 'The Media Inquiry Reports of the South African Human Rights Commission: A Critique'(2000) 99 *African Affairs* 373–93.

Global Policy Forum, 'NGOs and the United Nations. Comments for the Report of the Secretary General' June 1999, http://www.globalpolicy.org.

GLOPPEN, S, *South Africa: The Battle Over the Constitution* (Dartmouth, Ashgate, 1997).

GOMEZ, M, 'Sri Lanka's New Human Rights Commission'(1998) 20(2) *Human Rights Quarterly* 281–302.

—— 'Social Economic Rights and Human Rights Commissions'(1995) 17(1) *Human Rights Quarterly* 155–69.

GORDENKER, L, and WEISS, TG, 'NGO Participation in the International Policy Process'(1995) 16 *Third World Quarterly* 543.

GRANT, S, 'The NGO Role: Implementation, Expanding Protection and Monitoring the Monitors' in AF Bayefsky (ed), *The UN Human Rights Treaty System in the 21st Century* (Dordrecht, Kluwer Law International, 2000) 209–17.

GREEN, M, 'What We Talk About when We Talk About Indicators: Current Approaches to Human Rights Measurement' (2001) 23(4) *Human Rights Quarterly* 1062–97.

NFOR GWEI, S, 'The Cameroon Experience in Creating and Running a National Commission for the Promotion and Protection of Human Rights' in K Hossain et al, *Human Rights Commissions and Ombudsman Offices. National Experiences Throughout the World* (Dordrecht, Kluwer Law International, 2001) 169–86.

HADDEN, T, 'The Role of a National Commission in the Protection of Human Rights' in K Hossain et al (eds), *Human Rights Commissions and Ombudsman Offices* (Dordrecht, Kluwer Law International, 2001) 791–99.

HARDING, C, 'Statist Assumptions, Normative Individualism and New Forms of Personality: Evolving a Philosophy of International Law for the Twenty First Century' (2001) 1 *Non-State Actors and International Law* 197–125.

HATCHARD, J, 'National Human Rights Commissions in the Commonwealth', background paper to the Conference on Commonwealth Human Rights Institutions: Promoting Good Practice, organised by the Commonwealth Human Rights Initiative/Institute for Public Policy Research, 16–17 October 1997, London, UK.

Hatchard, J, 'A New Breed of Institution: The Development of Human Rights Commissions in Commonwealth Africa with particular Reference to the Uganda Human Rights Commission' (1999) *Comparative and International Law Journal of South Africa* 28.

—— *Workshop on the Use of Public Inquiries and Formal Hearings by Commonwealth Human Rights Commissions.* Report. Organised by British Council and the Uganda Human Rights Commission, 25–27 February 2003.

Hatchard, J, Ndulo, M, and Slinn, P, Comparative Constitutionalism and Good Governance in the Commonwealth: An Eastern and Southern African Perspective (Cambridge, Cambridge University Press, 2004).

Higgins, R, *Problems and Process: International Law and How We Use It* (Oxford, Oxford University Press, 1994).

Higgott, RA, Underhill, G, and Bieler, A, (eds), *Non-State Actors and Authority in the Global System* (London, Routledge, 2000).

Holm, JD, Molutsi, PP, and Somolekae, G, 'The Development of Civil Society in a Democratic State: The Botswana Model' (1996) 39(2) *African Studies Review* 43–69.

Hossain, K, Besselink, L, Selaisse, H, and Volker, E, (eds), *National Human Rights Commissions and Ombudsman Offices: National Experiences Throughout the World* (Dordrecht, Kluwer Law International, 2001).

House of Lords Select Committee on the Constitution, *The Regulatory State: Ensuring its Accountability*, 6th Report of Session 2003–04, HL Paper 68-I, 6 May 2004.

Howes, M, 'NGOs and the Development of Local Instituitons: A Ugandan Case Study'(1997) 35(1) *Journal of Modern African Studies* 17–35.

Hucker, J, 'Antidiscrimination Laws in Canada: Human Rights Commissions and the Search for Equality'(1997) 19(3) *Human Rights Quarterly* 547–71.

Human Rights Watch, *Protectors or Pretenders? Government Human Rights Commissions in Africa* (New York, Human Rights Watch, 2001).

Human Rights Watch, 'UN: New Council Must Champion Fight for Rights', 10 May 2006, http://hrw.org/english/docs/2006/05/10/global13343.htm.

Idike, C, 'Deflectionism or Activism? The Kenyan National Commission on Human Rights in Focus' (2004) 1(1) *Essex Human Rights Review* 40–53.

International Council on Human Rights Policy, *Performance and Legitimacy: National Human Rights Institutions* (Geneva, International Council on Human Rights Policy, 2000).

International Council on Human Rights, *Assessing the Effectiveness of National Human Rights Institutions* (Geneva, International Council on Human Rights, Office of the UN High Commissioner for Human Rights, 2005).

Jordan L, and Van Tuijl, P, 'Political Responsibility in Transnational NGO Advocacy'(2000) 28(12) *World Development* 2051–65.

Kabir, AHM, 'Establishing National Human Rights Commissions in Asia: A Critical Analysis of the Processes and Prospects' (2001) 2 *Asia-Pacific Journal of Human Rights and Law* 1.

Kamminga, MT, 'The Evolving Status of NGOs under International Law: A Threat to the Inter-State System?' in P Alston, *Non-State Actors and Human Rights* (Oxford, Oxford University Press, 2005) 93–112.

Keck, ME, and Sikkink, K, 'Transnational Advocacy Networks in International and Regional Politics' (New York, UNESCO 1999).

KOVACH, H, NELIGAN, C, and BURALL, S, *Power Without Accountability* (One World Trust, 2002/2003).

KUMAR, CR, 'National Human Rights Institutions: Good Governance Perspectives on Institutionalization of Human Rights' (2003) 2 *American University International Law Review* 259–300.

LEHR-LEHNARDT, R, 'NGO Legitimacy: Reassessing Democracy, Accountability and Transparency' 2005, Cornell Law School LLM Paper Series, Paper 6, http://lsr.nellco.org/cornell/lps/clacp/6.

LINDSNAES, B, LINDHOLT, L, and YIGEN, K, *National Human Rights Institutions. Articles and Working Papers* (Copenhagen, Danish Centre for Human Rights, 2000).

LIVINGSTONE, S, and MURRAY, R, *Evaluating the Effectiveness of National Human Rights Institutions. The Northern Ireland Human Rights Commission and Comparisons with South Africa*, 2005.

—— —— 'The Effectiveness of National Human Rights Institutions' in S Halliday and P Schmidt, *Human Rights Brought Home: Socio Legal Perspectives on Human Rights in the National Context* (Oxford, Hart Publishing, 2004) 137–64.

LIVINGSTONE, S, 'The Northern Ireland Human Rights Commission' (1999) 22 *Fordham International Law Journal* 1465–98.

LORD, R, 'The Liability of Non-State Actors for Torture in Violation of International Humanitarian Law: An Assessment of the Jurisprudence of the International Criminal Tribunal for the Former Yugoslavia' (2003) *Melbourne Journal of International Law* 112.

MCAUSLAN, P, 'Good Governance and Aid in Africa' (1996) 40(2) *Journal of African Law* 168–82.

MCCORQUODALE, R, 'The Individual and the International Legal System' in M Evans, *International Law* (Oxford, Oxford University Press, 2003) 299–325.

MAKUBUYA, A, 'Breaking the Silence: A Review of the Maiden Report of the Uganda Human Rights Commission' (1999) 5 *East African Journal of Peace and Human Rights* 213.

MALLESON, K, *The New Judiciary. The Effects of Expansion and Activism* (Dartmouth, Ashgate, 1999).

—— 'Safeguarding Judicial Impartiality'(2002) 22(1) *Legal Studies* 53–70.

MARAGIA, B, 'Almost There: Another way of Conceptualizing and Explaining NGOs Quest for Legitimacy in Global Politics' (2002) 2 *Non-State Actors and International Law* 301–32.

MATSHEKGA, J, 'Toothless Bulldogs? The Human Rights Commissions of Uganda and South Africa: A Comparative Study of their Independence' (2002) 2(1) *African Human Rights Law Journal* 68–91.

MENON, PK, 'The International Personality of Individuals in International Law: A Broadening of the Traditional Doctrine' (1992) 1 *Journal of Transnational Law and Policy* 151.

MOHIT, A, Report on the 7th session of the Ad Hoc Committee on the Comprehensive and Integral International Convention on the Protection and Promotion of the Rights and Dignity of Persons with Disabilities, New York.

MONGA, C, 'Civil Society and Democratisation in Francophone Africa' (1995) 33(3) *Journal of Modern African Studies* 359–79.

MUCHLINSKI, P, *Multinational Enterprises and the Law* (London, Blackwell, 1999).

MURRAY, R, 'Report of the 1999 Sessions of the African Commission on Human and Peoples' Rights' (2001) 22 *Human Rights Law Journal* 172–98.

MURRAY, R, *Human Rights in Africa. From Organization of African Unity to African Union* (Cambridge, Cambridge University Press, 2004).

MUTUNGA, W, and MAZRUI, A, 'Rights Integration in an Institutional Context: The Experience of the Kenya Human Rights Commission' (2002) 8 *Buffalo HRLR* 123.

National Human Rights Commission of Nigeria, *Statutory Report of the National Human Rights Commission for the Year 2003*. Presented by the Executive Secretary Bukhari Bello at the 2003 Annual Bar Conference of the Nigerian Bar Association, 25–29 August 2003, http://www.nigeriarights.gov.ng/statu.html.

NOLLKAEMPER, A, 'Concurrence between Individual Responsibility and State Responsibility in International Law' (2003) 52 *ICLQ* 615–40.

NORCHI, C, 'The National Human Rights Commission of India as a Value-Creating Institution' in J Montgomery (ed), *Human Rights: Positive Policies in Asia and the Pacific Rim* (Hollis New Hampshire, Hollis Publishing Company, 1998).

OBE, AMO, 'Working with National Human Rights Commissions. The Experience of Nigeria' www.scu.edu.tw/hr/research_imgs/Ayo.pdf

OKAFOR, OC, 'Reconceiving "Third World" Legitimate Governance Struggles in our Time: Emergent Imperatives for Rights Activism' (2000) 6 *Buffalo Human Rights Law Review* 1.

—— and AGBAKWA, SC, 'On Legalism, Popular Agency and "Voices of Suffering": The Nigerian National Human Rights Commission in Context' (2002) 24 *Human Rights Quarterly* 662–720.

OLZ, MA, 'Non-Governmental Organisations in Regional Human Rights Systems' (1997) 28 *Columbian Human Rights Law Review* 307.

PAUL, JA, 'NGOs and Global Policy-Making' Global Policy Forum, June 2000, http://www.globalpolicy.org.

PITYANA, B, 'South Africa's Inquiry into Racism in the Media: The Role of National Institutions in the Promotion and Protection of Human Rights' (2000) 99 *African Affairs* 525–32.

—— 'National Institutions at Work: The Case of the South African Human Rights Commission' in K Hossain, L Besselink, H Selassie and E Volker (eds), *Human Rights Commissions and Ombudsman Offices: National Experiences Throughout the World* (Dordrecht, Kluwer Law International, 2000).

POHJOLAINEN, A-E, *The Evolution of National Human Rights Institutions. The Role of the United Nations* (Danish Institute for Human Rights, Copenhagen, 2006)

POLLARD, M, 'Implementation of the Optional Protocol to the Convention against Torture and Other Cruel, Inhuman and Degrading Treatment or Punishment (OPCAT) in Federal and Decentralized States', Discussion Paper for the Seminar 'The Optional Protocol to the UN Convention Against Torture: Implementation in Federal States and Decentralized States' Sao Paulo, Brazil, 22–24 June 2005, www.apt.ch.

POSNER, MH, and WHITTOME, C, 'The Status of Human Rights NGOs' (1994) 25 *Columbian Human Rights Law Review* 269.

RATNER, S, 'Corporations and Human Rights: A Theory of Legal Responsibility' (2001) 11 *Yale Law Journal* 443.

RAZZAQUE, J, 'Changing Role of Friends of the Court in International Courts and Tribunals' (2002) 1 *Non-State Actors and International Law* 169–200.

Regional Conference on the Human Rights Dimensions of Corruption, the Nairobi Declaration, March 2006.

Reif, LC, 'Building Democratic Institutions: The Role of National Human Rights Institutions in Good Governance and Human Rights Protection' (2000) 13 *Harvard Human Rights Journal* 1–59.

Reinisch, A, 'The Changing International Legal Framework for Dealing with Non-State Actors' in P Alston, *Non-State Actors and Human Rights* (Oxford, Oxford University Press, 2005) 37–89.

Report of the Regional Conference for Africa, Dakar, 22–24 January 2001.

Reports of Preparatory Meetings and Activities at the International, Regional and National Levels, World Conference against Racism, Racial Discrimination, Xenophobia and Related Intolerance, 27 March 2001, A/CONF.189/PC.2/8.

Rubagotti, G, 'Non-Governmental Organisations and the Reporting Obligation under the International Covenant on Civil and Political Rights' (2005) 5 *Non-State Actors and International Law* 59–75.

Schabas, W, 'Theoretical and International Framework: Punishment of Non-State Actors in Non-International Armed Conflict' (2003) 26 *Fordham Journal of International Law* 907.

Scholte, JA, 'Civil Society and Democracy in Global Governance' (2002) 8 *Global Governance* 281–304.

Schreuer, C, 'The Waning of the Sovereign State: Towards a New Paradigm for International Law?' (1993) 4 *EJIL* 447–71.

Schweitz, ML, 'NGO Participation in International Governance: The Question of Legitimacy' (1995) 89 *American Society of International Law Proceedings* 415–20.

Scott, C, 'Accountability in the Regulatory State' (2000) 27(1) *Journal of Law and Society* 38–60.

Second International Workshop on National Institutions for the Promotion and Protection of Human Rights, Tunis, 13–17 December 1993.

Shelton, D, 'The Participation of Nongovernmental Organizations in International Judicial Proceedings' (1994) 88 *AJIL* 611.

Short, EF, 'The Development and Growth of Human Rights Commissions in Africa: The Ghanaian Experience' in K Hossain et al, *Human Rights Commissions and Ombudsman Offices. National Experiences Throughout the World* (Dordrecht, Kluwer Law International, 2001) 187–210.

Smith, J, and Pagnucco, R, with Lopez, GA, 'Globalising Human Rights: The Work of Transnational Human Rights NGOs in the 1990s' (1998) 20(2) *HRQ* 379–412.

Smith, N, 'Policing the Constitution' [1997] *Public Law* 234–44.

Statement by Morten Kjaerum, Director, Danish Institute for Human Rights. Chairperson International Coordinating Committee of National Institutions for the Promotion and Protection of Human Rights (ICC) at the 61st Session of the United Nations Commission on Human Rights, Geneva, April 2005.

Statement by National Human Rights Commission, Nigeria, at the Conference Against Racism, Racial Discrimination, Xenophobia and Related Intolerance, Durban South Africa, 31 August–7 September 2001, www.un.org/WCAR/statements/hr_com_nigeriaE.htm.

Statement at the Plenary by Dr Barney Pityana, Designated Spokesperson. Joint Statement of National Institutions, 4 September 2001, www.unhchr.ch.

Statement by Justice Elton Singini, SC, Law Commissioner/Human Rights Commissioner for Malawi at the 61st Session of the United Nations Commission on Human Rights, Geneva, April 2005.

Statement by Margaret Sekaggya, Chairperson, Uganda Human Rights Commission at the 61st Session of the United Nations Commission on Human Rights, Geneva, April 2005, www.nhri.net

Statement from the Coordinating Committee of African National Human Rights Institutions by Margaret Sekaggya, Chairperson, Uganda Human Rights Commission / Chairperson Coordinating Committee of the African National Human Rights Institutions at the 61st Session of the United Nations Commission on Human Rights, Geneva, April 2005.

Implementation of the Durban Programme of Action: An Exchange of Ideas on How to Move Forward. Seminar of Experts for the African Region, organised by the Office of the High Commissioner for Human Rights in Cooperation with the United Nations Office in Nairobi (UNON), 16–18 September 2002, http://www.nhri.net/pdf/Nairobi-Recommendations.pdf.

SYNDER, F, 'Governing Economic Globalisation: Global Legal Pluralism and European Law' (1999) 5(4) *European Law Journal* 334–74.

TABIU, M, 'National Human Rights Commission of Nigeria' in K Hossain et al, *Human Rights Commissions and Ombudsman Offices. National Experiences Throughout the World* (Dordrecht, Kluwer Law International, 2001) 553–59.

VON TIGERSTROM, B, 'The Role of the Ombudsman in Protecting Economic, Social and Cultural Rights' (1998) 2 *International Ombudsman Yearbook* 3–56.

TRIMBLE, PR, 'Globalization, International Institutions and the Erosion of National Sovereignty and Democracy' (1997) 95(6) *Michigan Law Review* 1944–69.

TSEKOS, ME, 'Human Rights Institutions in Africa' (2002) 9(2) *Human Rights Brief* 21–24.

UVIN, P, 'Scaling up the Grassroots and Scaling Down the Summit: The Relations between Third World Non-Governmental Organisations and the United Nations' (1995) 15 *Third World Quarterly* 495.

VAN BOVEN, T, 'The Role of Non-Governmental Organisations in International Human Rights Standard Setting: A Prerequisite for Democracy' (1990) 20 *California Western ILJ* 207.

DE WILDE, J, 'Flagging Democracy' (2004) 17(2) *International Journal for the Semiotics of Law* 211.

DE WAAL, A, 'Human Rights in Africa: Values, Institutions and Opportunities' in K Hossain et al, *Human Rights Commissions and Ombudsman Offices. National Experiences Throughout the World* (Dordrecht, Kluwer Law International, 2001) 759–81.

WARBRICK, C, 'States and Recognition in International Law' in M Evans, *International Law* (Oxford, Oxford University Press, 2003).

WEISSBRODT, D, 'The Role of International Non-Governmental Organizations in the Implementation of Human Rights' (1977) 12 *Tex. ILJ* 279.

WHITING, A, 'Situating Suhakam. Human Rights Debates and Malaysia's National Human Rights Commission' (2002) 39 *Stanford Journal of International Law* 1.

WILLETTS, P, 'Transnational Actors and International Organizations in Global Politics', in JB Baylis and S Smith (eds), *The Globalisation of World Politics*, (Oxford and New York, Oxford University Press, 2nd edn, 2001) 356–83.

DOCUMENTS OF INTERNATIONAL AND REGIONAL ORGANISATIONS

African National Human Rights Institutions

Rules of Procedure of the Coordinating Committee of African National Institutions for the Promotion and Protection of Human Rights.
First Conference of African National Human Rights Institutions (ANHRIs), Yaoundé, Cameroon, 5–7 February 1996, Yaoundé Declaration.
Second Conference of African National Human Rights Institutions, Durban, South Africa, 1–3 July 1998, Durban Declaration.
Third Conference of African National Human Rights Institutions, Lomé, Togo, 14–16 March 2001, Lomé Declaration.
Fourth Conference of African National Human Rights Institutions, Kampala, Uganda, 14–16 August 2002, Kampala Declaration.
Fifth Conference of African National Human Rights Institutions, Abuja, Nigeria, 8–10 November 2005, Abuja Declaration.
Final Report of Activities of the Fifth Conference of African National Human Rights Institutions Abuja, Nigeria, 8–11 November 2005, on file with author.
Meeting of the Coordinating Committee of African National Human Rights Institutions (ACCANI) and its Secretariat, Geneva, Switzerland, 12 April 2005, www.nrhi.net.

African Commission on Human and Peoples' Rights (ACHPR)

African Commission on Human and Peoples' Rights, Resolution on the Establishment of Committees on Human Rights or Other Similar Organs at National, Regional or Sub-Regional Level, Second Annual Report of the African Commission on Human and Peoples' Rights, Annex VIII
Recommendation on Some Modalities for Promoting Human and Peoples' Rights, Second Annual Report of the African Commission on Human and Peoples' Rights, Annex IX
Draft Resolution on Promotional Activities, Fifth Annual Report of the African Commission on Human and Peoples' Rights, Annex X
Conclusions and Recommendations of the Seminar on the National Implementation of the African Charter on Human and Peoples' Rights in the Internal Legal Systems in Africa, Banjul, The Gambia, 26–30 October 1992, Sixth Annual Report of the African Commission on Human and Peoples' Rights, Annex VIII.
Resolution on the African Commission on Human and Peoples' Rights, Sixth Annual Report of the African Commission on Human and Peoples' Rights.
Draft Concluding Observations on the Periodic Report of the Islamic Republic of Mauritania, on file with author.
African Commission on Human and Peoples' Rights, Zimbabwe. Report of the Fact Finding Mission, June 2002, DOC/OS (XXXIV)/346a.
Agenda of the 21st session of the African Commission, Doc.OS/7(XXI) Add.9.
Final Communiqué of the 21st Ordinary Session of the African Commission on Human and Peoples' Rights, Nouakchott, 15–24 April 1997.

Final Communiqué of the 22nd Ordinary Session of the African Commission on Human and Peoples' Rights, Banjul, 2–11 November 1997.

Resolution on the Human Rights Situation in Africa, 13th Annual Report of the ACHPR, Annex IV.

African Commission, Agenda of the 24th Ordinary Session, 12th Annual Activity Report of the African Commission on Human and Peoples' Rights, 1998–1999, AHG/215 (XXXV), Annex II.

Agenda of the 25th Ordinary Session, 12th Annual Activity Report of the African Commission on Human and Peoples' Rights, 1998–1999, AHG/215 (XXXV), Annex II.

Resolution on the Granting of Observer Status to National Human Rights Institutions in Africa (1998), ACHPR / Res.31(XXIV)98, October 1998.

Eleventh Annual Report of the African Charter on Human and Peoples' Rights, 1997–1998.

Grand Bay (Mauritius) Declaration and Plan of Action, 12–16 April 1999.

Final Communiqué of the 32nd Ordinary Session of the African Commission on Human and Peoples' Rights, Banjul, The Gambia, 17–23 October 2002.

Draft Report of the Consultative Meeting between the African Commission on Human and People's Rights and the United Nations High Commissioner for Refugees, Addis Ababa, Ethiopia, 20–21 March 2003.

Final Communiqué of the 33rd Ordinary Session of the African Commission on Human and Peoples' Rights, Niamey, Niger, 15–29 April 2003.

Resolution on Guidelines and Measures for the Prohibition and Prevention of Torture, Cruel, Inhuman or Degrading Treatment of Punishment in Africa.

African Commission on Human and Peoples' Rights, Pretoria Declaration on Economic, Social and Cultural Rights

Kigali Declaration, 8 May 2003.

Final Communiqué of the 34th Ordinary Session of the African Commission on Human and Peoples' Rights, Banjul, The Gambia, 6–20 November 2003.

Final Communiqué of the 36th Ordinary Session of the African Commission on Human and Peoples' Rights, Dakar, Senegal, 23 November–7 December 2004.

African Commission on Human and Peoples' Rights, First meeting of the Follow Up Committee on Robben Island Guidelines, 19–20 February 2005.

African Union (AU)

Statutes of the Economic, Social and Cultural Council, PRC/ECOSOCC Statutes/Rev.5.

Protocol to the African Charter on Human and Peoples' Rights Establishing an African Court on Human and Peoples' Rights, 1998.

Decision on the Seats of the African Union, Assembly/AU/Dec.45(III).

Decision on the Merger of the African Court on Human and Peoples' Rights and the Court of Justice of the African Union, Assembly/AU/Dec.83 (V).

Decision on the Election of the Judges of the African Court on Human and Peoples' Rights, Assembly/AU/Dec.100 (VI).

Report of the Retreat of Members of the African Commission on Human and Peoples' Rights (ACHPR) facilitated by the Office of the High Commissioner for Human Rights (OHCHR), African Union Conference Centre, Addis Ababa, Ethiopia, 24–26 September 2003.

First African Union Conference of National Human Rights Institutions, Addis Ababa, 18–21 October 2004, Draft Report, on file with author.

Final Communiqué of the First African Union Conference of National Human Rights Institutions, Addis Ababa, Ethiopia, 18–21 October 2004.
Draft Report on the First African Union Conference of National Human Rights Institutions, Addis Ababa, Ethiopia, 18–21 October 2004, on file with author.
Draft Protocol on the Statute of the African Court of Justice and Human Rights, May 2006, EX.CL/211 (VIII) Rev.1, Annex II

United Nations (UN)

Articles on the Responsibility of States for Internationally Wrongful Acts, UN Doc.A/56/10 (2001), as approved by the General Assembly, Res.56/83 (2001).
Rules of Procedure of the General Assembly, A/520/Rev.15, 1985.
Rules of Procedure of World Conference, Rule 65, A/CONF.189/92.
Principles Relating to the Status and Functioning of National Institutions for the Protection and Promotion of Human Rights (The Paris Principles), Resolution 1992/54, endorsed by UN General Assembly Resolution 48/134, 20 December 1993, Annex.
Declaration on the Right and Responsibilities of Individuals, Groups, and Organs of Society to Promote and Protect Universally Recognized Human Rights and Fundamental Freedoms, UN GA 1999, GA Res.53/144 (1999).
United Nations Office of the High Commissioner for Human Rights (OHCHR), National Institutions Programme, African Region. National Institutions Regional Activities–Update, September 2003.
United Nations Office of the High Commissioner for Human Rights (OHCHR), Africa Region, Quarterly Reports of Field Offices, March 2005.
UN OHCHR, First Quarterly Public Report for 2005, National Institutions Activities, January–March 2005.
United Nations, *National Human Rights Institutions. A Handbook on the Establishment and Strengthening of National Institutions for the Promotion and Protection of Human Rights, Professional Training Series No 4*, 1995.
United Nations, Report of the Secretary General, *Further Promotion and Encouragement of Human Rights and Fundamental Freedoms, Including the Question of the Programme and Methods of Work of the Commission. National Institutions for the Promotion and Protection of Human Rights*, E/CN.4/1993/33, 5 January 1993.
Report of the Secretary-General, Human Rights Questions: Human Rights Questions, including Alternative Approaches for Improving the Effective Enjoyment of Human Rights and Fundamental Freedoms, National Institutions for the Promotion and Protection of Human Rights, 20 September 1995, A/50/452.
United Nations, *Enhancing the Participation of National Human Rights Institutions in the Work of the Commission on Human Rights and its Subsidiary Bodies, Report of the Secretary General,* 19 January 2005, E/CN.4/2005/107.
Resolution 50/176, National Institutions for the Promotion and Protection of Human Rights, 22 December 1995.
United Nations, ECOSOC Decision 1997/253, National Institutions for the Promotion and Protection of Human Rights.
United Nations, ECOSOC Decision 1998/258, National Institutions for the Promotion and Protection of Human Rights.

Resolution 52/128, United Nations, National Institutions for the Promotion and Protection of Human Rights, 26 February 1998.

Resolution 54/176, United Nations, National Institutions for the Promotion and Protection of Human Rights, A/RES/54/176, 15 February 2000.

Resolution 56/158, United Nations, National Institutions for the Promotion and Protection of Human Rights, 15 February 2002.

Resolution 58/175, United Nations, National Institutions for the Promotion and Protection of Human Rights, 10 March 2004.

Committee on Economic, Social and Cultural Rights, List of Issues: Libyan Arab Jamahiriya, 14 December 2004, E/C.12/Q/LBY/1, para 3.

Committee on Economic, Social and Cultural Rights, General Comment No.10, 1989.

Concept Paper on the High Commissioner's Proposal for a Unified Standing Treaty Body, Report by the Secretariat, HRI/MC/2006/CRP.1, 14 March 2006.

UN, *Principles Relating to the Status and Functioning of National Institutions for Protection and Promotion of Human Rights*, Report E/CN.4/1992/43.

UN, *Further Promotion and Encouragement of Human Rights and Fundamental freedoms, including the Question of the Programme and methods of Work of the Commission, National Institutions for the Promotion and Protection of Human Rights*, E/CN.4/1993/33, 5 January 1993.

National Institutions for the Promotion and Protection of Human Rights, Commission on Human Rights Resolution 1993/55, E/CN.4/RES/1993/55, 9 March 1993.

National Institutions for the Promotion and Protection of Human Rights, Commission on Human Rights Resolution 1994/54, E/CN.4/RES/1994/54, 4 March 1994.

UN, *Effective Functioning of Human Rights Mechanism: National Institutions for the Promotion and Protection of Human Rights. Report of the SG submitted in accordance with Commission on Human Rights Resolution 1998/55*, E/CN.4/1999/95, 3 February 1995.

UN, *Human Rights Questions: Human Rights Questions, including Alternative Approaches for Improving the Effective Enjoyment of Human Rights and Fundamental Freedoms, National Institutions for the Promotion and Protection of Human Rights, Report of the Secretary General*, A/50/452, 20 September 1995.

UN, *National Human Rights Institutions. A Handbook on the Establishment and Strengthening of National Institutions for the Promotion and Protection of Human Rights*, Professional Training Series No 4, 1995.

UN, *Further Promotion and Encouragement of Human Rights and Fundamental Freedoms, including the Question of the Programme and Methods of Work of the Commission, National Institutions for the Promotion and Protection of Human Rights, Report by the Secretary General submitted in accordance with Commission on Human Rights Resolution 1996/50*, E/CN.4/1997/51, 5 February 1997.

Enhancing the Participation of National Human Rights Institutions in the Work of the Commission on Human Rights and its Subsidiary Bodies, Report of the Secretary General, 19 January 2005, E/CN.4/2005/107.

United Nations, Commission on Human Rights, *Effective Functioning of Human Rights Mechanisms: National Institutions and Regional Arrangements*, E/CN.4/2005/L.92/Rev.1, 19 April 2005.

UN, *Enhancing the Participation of National Human Rights Institutions in the Work of the Commission on Human Rights and its Subsidiary Bodies, Report of the Secretary General*, 19 January 2005, E/CN.4/2005/107.

Commission on Human Rights, National Institutions for the Promotion and Protection of Human Rights, Resolution 2005/74, 59th meeting, 20 April 2005.

Commission on Human Rights, *Effective Functioning of Human Rights Mechanisms: National Institutions and Regional Arrangements, Report of the Secretary-General*, 24 January 2006, E/CN.4/2006/101.

Commission on Human Rights, *Effective Functioning of Human Rights Mechanisms: National Institutions and Regional Arrangements, Process Currently Utilized by the International Coordinating Committee to Accredit national Human Rights Institutions in Compliance with the Paris Principles and ensure that the process is strengthened with appropriate periodic review and on ways and means of enhancing the participation of national human rights institutions in the work of the Commission, Report of the Secretary-General*, 25 January 2006, E/CN.4/2006/102.

Commission on Human Rights, *Effective Functioning of Human Rights Mechanisms: National Institutions and Regional Arrangements, Information Presented by the Asia Pacific Forum of National Human Rights Institutions, Note by the Secretariat*, 24 March 2006, E/CN.4/2006/NI/1.

Human Rights Council, *Report to the General Assembly on the Third Session of the Human Rights Council, Draft Report of the Council*, A/HRC/3/L.11, 8 December 2006

Report of the UN High Commissioner for Human Rights to the Economic and Social Council, 29 June 2000, E/2000/83.

OHCHR, An Optional Protocol to the International Covenant on Economic, Social and Cultural Rights. Note for National Human Rights Institutions, 2006, on file with author.

UN OHCHR, Member States Meeting Geneva, 28–29 June 2004. National Institutions Activities, January–June 2004, 16 June 2004.

Report of the United Nations High Commissioner for Human Rights and Follow up to the World Conference on Human Rights, *Effective Functioning of Human Rights Mechanisms, Note by the United Nations High Commissioner for Human Rights*, 5 July 2004, E/CN.4/2005/5.

Commission on Human Rights, *Effective Functioning of Human Rights Mechanisms: National Institutions and Regional Arrangements*, 19 April 2005, E/CN.4/2005/L.92/Rev.1.

Draft Harmonized Guidelines on Reporting under the International Human Rights Treaties, including Guidelines on a Common Core Document and Treaty-Specific Targeted Documents, 1 June 2005, HRI/MC/2005/3.

General Recommendation XVII on the Establishment of National Institutions to Facilitate Implementation of the Convention, 25 March 1993. Resolution 58/175, National Institutions for the Promotion and Protection of Human Rights, 10 March 2004.

General Comment No 2, The Role of Independent National Human Rights Institutions in the Promotion and Protection of the Rights of the Child, 31st session, 2002, HRI/GEN/1/Rev.7.

General Recommendation XVII on the Establishment of National Institutions to Facilitate Implementation of the Convention, 25 March 1993.

Committee on the Elimination of Racial Discrimination in its Concluding Observations on the state report of Côte d'Ivoire, 62nd session, CERD/C/62/CO/1, 3 June 2003.

Concluding Observations of the Committee on the Elimination of Racial Discrimination in respect of Chad's 2003 report, A/48/18, 42nd session of the CERD Committee.

Concluding Observations on Zimbabwe's report at its 56th session, Committee on the Elimination of Racial Discrimination, CERD/C/304/Add.92, 19 April 2000.

Concluding Observations on Rwanda at its 56th session, Committee on the Elimination of Racial Discrimination, CERD/C/304/Add.97, 19 April 2000.

Concluding Observations on Mauritius at its 57th session, Committee on the Elimination of Racial Discrimination, CERD/C/304/Add.106, 1 May 2001, para 10.

Concluding Observations on Algeria at its 58th session, Committee on the Elimination of Racial Discrimination, CERD/C/304/Add.113, 27 April 2001.

Concluding Observations on Egypt at its 59th session, Committee on the Elimination of Racial Discrimination, A/56/18.

Concluding Observations on Sudan at its 23rd session, Committee on Economic, Social and Cultural Rights, E/C.12/1/Add.48, 1 September 2000.

Concluding Observations on Togo at its 25th session, Committee on Economic, Social and Cultural Rights E/C.12/1/Add.61, 21 May 2001.

Committee on Economic, Social and Cultural Rights, Concluding Observations of the Committee on Economic, Social and Cultural Rights: Sudan, 1 September 2000, E/C.12/1/Add.48.

Gabon's second periodic report before the Human Rights Committee, Human Rights Committee, List of Issues: Gabon, 17/08/2000, CCPR/C/70/L/GAB, 17 August 2000.

Concluding Observations on Egypt at its 22nd session, Committee on Economic, Social and Cultural Rights, E/C.12/1/Add.44, 23 May 2000.

Committee on the Rights of the Child, Concluding Observations of the Committee on the Rights of the Child, Côte d'Ivoire, 9 July 2001, CRC/C/15/Add.155.

Committee on the Rights of the Child, Concluding Observations of the Committee on the Rights of the Child, Tunisia, 16 June 2002, CRC/C/15/Add.181.

Committee on the Rights of the Child, Concluding Observations of the Committee on the Rights of the Child, Egypt, 21 February 2001, CRC/C/15/Add.145.

Committee on the Rights of the Child, List of Issues: Equatorial Guinea, 11 June 2004, CRC/C/Q/GNQ/1.

Committee on the Rights of the Child, List of Issues: Sao Tome and Principe, 13 February 2004, CRC/C/Q/STP/1.

Committee on the Rights of the Child, Concluding Observations of the Committee on the Rights of the Child, Cape Verde, 7 November 2001, CRC/C/15/Add.168.

Concluding Observations on Cameroon's state report, the Committee Against Torture, 25th session, A/56/44.

Concluding Observations on Mali at its 77th session, Human Rights Committee, CCPR/CO/77/MLI, 16 April 2003.

Concluding Observations on Malawi at its 63rd session, Committee on the Elimination of Racial Discrimination, CERD/C/63/CO/12, 10 December 2003.

Committee on the Rights of the Child, Concluding Observations of the Committee on the Rights of the Child: Kenya, 7 November 2001, CRC/C/15/Add.160.

General Recommendation XXVIII on the follow-up to the World Conference Against Racism, Racial Discrimination, Xenophobia and Related Intolerance, 60th session, CERD Committee, 2002, HRI/GEN/1/Rev.7.

General Comment Adopted by the Committee on the Rights of the Child, 26th session, 2001, General Comment No 1: The Aims of Education.

CEDAW General Recommendation No 6, 7th session, 1988, Effective National Machinery and Publicity.

ECOSOC decision 2004/14, Comprehensive and Integral International Convention on Protection and Promotion of the Rights and Dignity of Persons with Disabilities.

Resolution ECOSOC 1996/31, UN Doc.E/1996/31, 25 July 1996.

Mission to Thailand, Report Submitted by the Special Representative of the Secretary General on the Situation of Human Rights Defenders, Hina Jilani, E/CN.4/2004/94/ Add.1, 12 March 2004.

Report of the Special Representative of the Secretary General on Human Rights Defenders, A/57/182, 2 July 2002.

Press Release. National Human Rights Institutions Outline their Work to Commission on Human Rights, 13 April 2005, www.unhchr.ch.

United Nations, Draft International Code of Conduct on Transnational Corporations, 23 ILM (1984) 626.

UN Sub-Commission on the Promotion and Protection of Human Rights, Norms on the Responsibilities of Transnational Corporations and Other Business Enterprises with Regard to Human Rights, E/CN.4/Sub.2/2003/12/Rev.2.

Observance by United Nations Forces of International Humanitarian Law, United Nations, Secretary-General's bulletin, ST/SGB/1999/13, 6 August 1999, 36 ILM (1999) 1656.

International Coordinating Committee of National Human Rights Institutions (ICC) and National Institutions Unit (NI Unit)

International Coordinating Committee of National Institutions for the Promotion and Protection of Human Rights, Rules of Procedure, www.nhri.net.

Rules of Procedure of the ICC Sub-Committee on Accreditation, as adopted by the members of the International Coordinating Committee at its 15th session, Seoul, Republic of Korea, 14 September 2004, www.nhri.net.

International Coordinating Committee of National Human Rights Institutions for the Promotion and Protection of Human Rights, *Report and Recommendations of the Sub-Committee on Accreditation*, 18th Session Santa Cruz, 27 October 2006, www.nhri.net

International Coordinating Committee Working Group on Accreditation, *Discussion Paper on the Review of ICC Accreditation Procedures for National Human Rights Institutions (NHRI)*, September 2006, www.nhri.net.

International Coordinating Committee of National Human Rights Institutions (ICC), *ICC Position Papers. National Human Rights Institutions and the UN Human Rights Council, Volume I*, 27 June 2006, www.nhri.net.

International Coordinating Committee of National Human Rights Institutions (ICC), *ICC Position Papers. National Human Rights Institutions and the UN Human Rights Council, Volume II: National Human Rights Institutions and the Special Procedures and Universal Periodic Review Mechanism*, 22 September 2006, www.nhri.net.

Opening Statement by Morten Kjaerum, Chairperson, International Coordinating Committee of National Institutions for the Promotion and Protection of Human Rights (ICC), at the 17th session of the Annual meeting of the ICC, Geneva, 12 April 2006, on file with author.

Draft Report of the 16th Session of the International Coordinating Committee of National Institutions for the Promotion and Protection of Human Rights (ICC), 14–16 April 2006, on file with author.

ICC, Draft Report on ICC Activities 2005–2006, 17th Session of the International Coordinating Committee of NHRIs, 10–11 April 2006.

ICC, Discussion Paper on NHRIs in the UN Reform Process, 17th session of the International Coordinating Committee of NHRIs, on file with author.

ICC, Report and Recommendations of the Sub-Committee on Accreditation, 17th session of the International Coordinating Committee of NHRIs, 10–11 April 2006, on file with author.

ICC, Draft Proposal for ICC Re-Accreditation Procedures for NHRIs, 17th session of the International Coordinating Committee of NHRIs, 1—11 April 2006, on file with author.

ICC, Draft Report on ICC Activities 2005–2006, 17th session of the International Coordinating Committee of NHRIs, 10–11 April 2006, on file with author.

ICC, Draft ICC Work Plan 2006, 17th session of the International Coordinating Committee of NHRIs, 10–11 April 2006, on file with author.

ICC, National Institutions in Need: Guidelines for Early Warning, on file with author.

'Strengthening the Implementation of Human Rights treaty recommendations through the enhancement of national protection measures,' Participation of the National Institutions Unit in the Treaty Body Recommendations Follow-Up Project, Annual Meeting of the ICC, April 2005, www.nhri.net

NI Unit, *The United Nations Treaty Bodies and National Institutions*, http://www.nhri.net/pdf/TBs_and_NIs.pdf.

17th session of the International Coordinating Committee of NHRIs, Agenda item 9a–9d. The Role of NHRIs in the UN System. Discussion Paper on NHRIs in the UN Reform Process.

Report and Recommendations of the Sub-Committee on Accreditation, International Coordinating Committee of National Human Rights Institutions for the Promotion and Protection of Human Rights, 16th Session, Geneva, 14–15 April 2005.

Other Regional Bodies

Council of Europe, Committee of Ministers, Resolution No R (97) 14, of the Committee of Ministers to Member States on the Establishment of Independent National Human Rights Institutions, adopted 30 September 1997, http://www.nhri.net/pdf/CoeRecommendation1997no14.pdf.

Council of Europe Committee of Ministers, Resolution (97)11 on Co-operation between National Human Rights Institutions of Member States and Between them and the Council of Europe, adopted 30 September 1997, see http://www.nhri.net/pdf/CoeResolution1997no11.pdf.

OAS, *Declaration on Support for the Work of Defenders of the People, Defenders of the Population, Human Rights Attorneys, and Human Rights Commissioners (Ombudsmen) in the Context of Strengthening Democracy in the Hemisphere*, OAS General Assembly, Support for the Work of Defenders of the People, Defenders of the Population, Human Rights Attorneys, and Human Rights Commissioners (Ombudsmen) in the Context of Strengthening Democracy in the Hemisphere, OAS AG/RES 1601, XXVIII-O/98 (1998).

OAS Support for the Work of Defenders of the People, Defenders of the Population, Human Rights Attorneys and Human Rights Commissioners (Ombudsmen) in the Context of Strengthening Democracy in the Hemisphere, adopted at first plenary session, 7 June 1999, AG/RES.1670 (XXIX-0/99); Support for International Exchanges of Experience Among Ombudsmen, adopted at 7th plenary session, 5 June 1997, AG/RES.1505 (XXVII-0/97).

Copenhagen Declaration from the Sixth International Conference for National Institutions for the Promotion and Protection of Human Rights (Copenhagen and Lund, 10–13 April 2002).

Paper of the Australian EOC to the 9th Annual Meeting of Asia Pacific Forum on NHRIs on 'The Role of NIs in the United Nations Commission on the Status of Women.'

OECD, Guidelines for Multinational Enterprises, 21 June 1976, 15 ILM (1976) 969.

Index